Praise for HUNDREDS OF HEADS® *Survival Guides:*

"Hundreds of Heads is an innovative publishing house. . . . Its entertaining and informative 'How To Survive...' series takes a different approach to offering advice. Thousands of people around the nation were asked for their firsthand experiences and real-life tips in six of life's arenas. Think 'Chicken Soup' meets 'Zagats,' says a press release, and rightfully so."
— ALLEN O. PIERLEONI, "BETWEEN THE LINES," THE SACRAMENTO BEE

"At some point, the Chick      is to run its course. . . . Here's our cont   e How to Survive series, published   Launched in 2004, the series flatly igno   but blunt advice from thousands across America who've walked some of life's rougher roads."
— LAURI GITHENS HATCH, ROCHESTER DEMOCRAT AND CHRONICLE

"The books have struck a nerve: Freshman Year was the No.1–selling college-life guide of 2004 . . ."
— TODD LEOPOLD, CNN.COM

"Hundreds of Heads Books hopes to make life in our complicated new millennium a bit more manageable. . . . Rather than approach a handful of psychologists or other so-called experts, the editors have polled hundreds of 'real people' who have gone through the challenges and lived to tell about them."
— BILL ERVOLINO, "BOOKMARKS," THE RECORD, HACKENSACK, NEW JERSEY

"A concept that will be . . . a huge seller and a great help to people. I firmly believe that today's readers want sound bytes of information, not tomes. Your series will most definitely be the next 'Chicken Soup.'"
— CYNTHIA BRIAN
TV/RADIO PERSONALITY, BEST SELLING AUTHOR: CHICKEN SOUP FOR THE GARDENER'S SOUL; BE THE STAR YOU ARE!; THE BUSINESS OF SHOW BUSINESS

"Move over, 'Dummies'. . . Can that 'Chicken Soup!' Hundreds of Heads are on the march to your local bookstore!"
— ELIZABETH HOPKINS,
KFNX (PHOENIX) RADIO HOST, THINKING OUTSIDE THE BOX

Advance Praise for

HOW TO LOSE 9,000 LBS. (OR LESS)

"Informative and entertaining… a must-read if you have ever struggled with the delicate 'D' word."
—ZORA ANDRICH
REALITY SHOW CONTESTANT

"For all of those people who say they've 'been there, done that' when it comes to dieting—this book actually goes there and does that, to show us how to be successful in our own quest for permanent weight loss."
—SUSIE GALVEZ
BEAUTY INDUSTRY EXPERT AND AUTHOR; LOST 120 LBS.

Praise for other titles in the HUNDREDS OF HEADS® *Survival Guide series:*

HOW TO SURVIVE YOUR TEENAGER

"Parents of teens and parents of kids approaching those years will find wisdom on each page...provides insight, humor, and empathy…"
—FOREWORD MAGAZINE, JULY/AUGUST 2005

"These anecdotes, written by people who have been there, hit the nail on the head! Some you'll recognize as wonderful suggestions or insightful descriptions of true-life experiences. Others will help you recognize traps to avoid. This book tells it like it is."
—STEVEN PERLOW, PH.D.
CLINICAL PSYCHOLOGIST, ATLANTA, GEORGIA

"Words of wisdom: Hundreds of parents nationwide weigh in with advice on everything from messy bedrooms to driving to sex…"
—THE CINCINNATI ENQUIRER

"As the owner of the largest prom Web site in the world, I deal with teens every day. But it took this book to really prepare me for the coming-into-teenhood of my own three boys. This book is a marvelous achievement! I whole-heartedly recommend it."
—RICHARD G. CALO, PH.D.
CREATOR OF THEPROMSITE.COM AND AUTHOR OF THE FIRST BOOK OF PROM

"With warmth, humor and 'I've been there' compassion, editors Gluck and Rosenfeld have turned the ordinary experiences and struggles of parents into bits of compact wisdom that are easy to pick up and use straightaway. I especially liked this book's many examples of how to survive (and even thrive) while living under the same roof as your teen."
—JACLYNN MORRIS, M.ED.
CO-AUTHOR OF I'M RIGHT. YOU'RE WRONG. NOW WHAT? AND FROM ME TO YOU

"The book really gave me some insight on my life and hopefully my parents will read it so we can improve our relationship."
—DAVID E. WEINSTEIN
10TH GRADE CLASS PRESIDENT, RIVERWOOD HIGH SCHOOL
SANDY SPRINGS, GEORGIA

HOW TO SURVIVE YOUR FRESHMAN YEAR

"This book proves that all of us are smarter than one of us."
—JOHN KATZMAN
FOUNDER AND CEO, PRINCETON REVIEW

"...a guide full of fantastic advice from hundreds of young scholars who've been there, as well as dropouts who reflect on their decision... It's a quick and fun read with short stories and quotes about the pros and cons of everything from getting a job during the school year to dating within your residence."
—BOSTON HERALD

"Voted in the Top 40 Young Adults books."
—PENNSYLVANIA SCHOOL LIBRARIANS ASSOCIATION

"Good advice about saying goodbye to your parents, dealing with homesickness, making new friends, and getting around campus. Should you live in a dorm or off campus? Oh, yeah, and what about studying? Alone or with groups? These questions and lots more (money, laundry, food, sex, parties, time-management, etc.) are addressed with honesty and humor. This would be a great book to have for the graduating high school seniors to make them less anxious about college."
—NORMA LILLY
M.L.S., INGRAM LIBRARY SERVICE, HIDDEN GEM

"This cool new book...helps new college students get a head start on having a great time and making the most of this new and exciting experience."

"Explains college to the clueless...This quick read is jam-packed with tidbits."

"This book is right on the money. I wish I had this before I started college."

HOW TO SURVIVE DATING

"Rated one of the Top 10 Dating Books."

"Reading this book, I laughed out loud... I also decided to decree snippets a most superior art form for dating manuals."

"Whether you're single or not, *How to Survive Dating* will have you rolling with laughter...This isn't your ordinary dating book."

"Invaluable advice... If I had read this book before I made my movie, it would have been only *10 Dates*."

"Reading *How to Survive Dating* is like having a big circle of friends in one room offering their hard-earned advice about the toughest dating dilemmas. From the first kiss to knowing when it's time to say 'I love you,' this book can help you avoid the headaches and heartaches of dating. *How to Survive Dating* is a must-read for singles."

"Great, varied advice, in capsule form, from the people who should know—those who've dated and lived to tell the tale."

"'Be yourself' may be good dating advice, but finding Mr. or Ms. Right usually takes more than that. For those seeking more than the typical trite suggestions, *How to Survive Dating* has dating tips from average folks across the country. It's like having a few hundred friends on speed-dial."
—KNIGHT RIDDER/TRIBUNE NEWS SERVICE (KRT)

"Hilarious!"
—TEENA JONES
THE TEENA JONES SHOW, *KMSR-AM (DALLAS)*

HOW TO SURVIVE A MOVE

"Hundreds of essential moving tips, real-life stories, and quotes by movers across the United States and Canada."
—LIBRARY JOURNAL

"As a realtor, I see the gamut of moving challenges. This book is great —covering everything from a 'heads-up' on the travails of moving to suggested solutions for the problems. AND... it's a great read!"
—JEANNE MOELLENDICK, *RE/MAX* SPECIALISTS, JACKSONVILLE, FLORIDA

"How to Survive A Move is full of common sense ideas and moving experiences from everyday people. I have been in the moving industry for 22 years and I was surprised at all the new ideas I learned from your book!"
—FRED WALLACE, PRESIDENT, ONE BIG MAN & ONE BIG TRUCK MOVING COMPANY

"Tidbits that are easy to digest when you're more concerned with packing boxes than spending hours reading a book."
—SAN DIEGO UNION-TRIBUNE

"The editors of *How to Survive A Move* went to the experts: average people who've been there and done that. Much of the advice is the kind you're unlikely to get from the experts—such as living east of where you work so you won't be driving into the sun, using T-shirts to pad breakable items, and making sure to pack, ahem, adult paraphernalia in a really, really well-sealed box."
—DEMOCRAT AND CHRONICLE (ROCHESTER, NEW YORK)

"Packed with some good moving advice."

"A good resource book for do-it-yourself movers to learn some of the best tips in making a move easier."

HOW TO SURVIVE YOUR MARRIAGE

"Simple tricks to help save your marriage."

"I love this book!"

"A unique offering and sorely needed resource of advice/wisdom from men and women who have found creative solutions to the many challenges of marriage and now are reaping its awards."

"How to Survive Your Marriage is a fun companion to research-based marriage manuals. Great for starting a discussion with your partner or laughing at the commonality of concerns that engaged couples often face."

"Reader-friendly and packed full of good advice. They should hand this out at the marriage license counter!"

"Full of honest advice from newlyweds and longtime couples. This book answers the question—'How do other people do it?'"

"This book is the best wedding present I received! It's great to go into a marriage armed with the advice of hundreds of people who have been through it all already."

HOW TO SURVIVE YOUR BABY'S FIRST YEAR

"Both informative and entertaining, this book is an excellent resource and companion book to other books on babies and parenting."
—PARENTS & KIDS MAGAZINE

"What to read when you're reading the other baby books. The perfect companion for your first-year baby experience."
—SUSAN REINGOLD, M.A., EDUCATOR

"As a new parent, it helps to know that you're not alone in facing one of life's biggest challenges. *How to Survive Your Baby's First Year* offers a compilation of humorous quotes from mothers and fathers who survived parenthood."
—LOS ANGELES DAILY NEWS

"*How to Survive Your Baby's First Year*...offers tried-and-true methods of baby care and plenty of insight to the most fretted about parenting topics..."
—BOOKVIEWS

"An amazing kaleidoscope of insights into surviving parenthood, this book will reassure moms and dads that they are not alone in the often scary world of bringing up baby."
—JOSEF SOLOWAY, M.D., F.A.A.P.
CLINICAL ASSOCIATE PROFESSOR OF PEDIATRICS
WEILL MEDICAL COLLEGE OF CORNELL UNIVERSITY

"Full of real-life ideas and tips. If you love superb resource books for being the best parent you can be, you'll love *How to Survive Your Baby's First Year.*"
—ERIN BRWON CONROY, M.A.
AUTHOR, COLUMNIST, MOTHER OF TWELVE, AND CREATOR OF TOTALLYFITMOM.COM

"The Hundreds of Heads folks have done it again! Literally hundreds of moms and dads from all over offer their nuggets of wisdom—some sweet, some funny, all smart—on giving birth, coming home and bringing up baby."
—ANDREA SARVADY
AUTHOR OF BABY GAMI

"You can keep the damn china!"

WARNING:

This guide contains differing
opinions. Hundreds of heads
will not always agree.
Advice taken in combination may
cause unwanted side effects. Use
your head when selecting advice.

"You can keep the damn china!"

And 824 Other Great Tips on Dealing with Divorce

ROBERT J. NACHSHIN AND JENNIFER BRIGHT REICH
SPECIAL EDITORS

Hundreds of Heads Books, LLC
ATLANTA

See page 226–227 for credits and permissions.

Library of Congress Cataloging-in-Publication Data

You can keep the damn china! : and 824 other great tips in dealing with divorce / Robert Nachshin, Jennifer Bright Reich, special editors.
   p. cm.
  ISBN-13: 978-0-9746292-6-1
  ISBN-10: 0-9746292-6-X
  1. Divorce. I. Nachshin, Robert. II. Reich, Jennifer Bright.
  HQ814.Y68 2006
  306.89--dc22
                2005031489

Cover photograph by PictureQuest

HUNDREDS OF HEADS® books are available at special discounts when purchased in bulk for premiums or institutional or educational use. Excerpts and custom editions can be created for specific uses. For more information, please email sales@hundredsofheads.com or write to:

HUNDREDS OF HEADS BOOKS, LLC
#230
2221 Peachtree Road, Suite D
Atlanta, Georgia 30309

ISBN-10: 0-9746292-6-X
ISBN-13: 978-097462926-1

Printed in U.S.A.
10 9 8 7 6 5 4 3 2 1

CONTENTS

Introduction

D ivorce is a very personal experience—a very individual one—
because the process itself differs from person to person. Some find
the life-altering event a relief, while others may suffer remorse and long-
ing. Whether *you* wanted the divorce or not, the "getting through it" still
remains a challenge because it is typically fraught with complex and difficult issues. And everyone has his or her own way of doing just that:
getting through it.

The chapters that lie ahead take some of the angst out of the divorce
process because they are presented in a way to help you understand
every step you'll go through. The contents of this book are not just a
compilation of comments from those who are divorced. Instead, the
chapters share real experiences, how-to's, do's and don'ts, and by passing
them on they provide sound advice, comfort and counsel from others just
like you—from those who have learned from "divorce mistakes" and
from those who have triumphed in spite of them.

Because this book culls information from a variety of sources, the
view of what works (and what doesn't) is broad. It would be almost
impossible *not* to relate to many of the instances you will read about.

While many of the divorce experiences are similar (you'll probably
say to yourself more than once, "I can relate."), there are still those that
may seem unique. The common ground for you and for those interviewed
is this: survival. That's the intent of the book.

As a reader you should feel free to use it as a reference book, a daily
guide or a practical precautionary measure against making future mistakes. It's one of those wonderful books that allow you to determine
what value it has to *you*.

ROBERT J. NACHSHIN

E ven though the American divorce rate has declined slightly since hitting its highest point in the early 1980s, the average couple's lifetime chance of divorce or separation remains close to 50 percent.

The good news is that you are not alone on this journey; roughly 20 percent of Americans—one out of every five—have been divorced.

They've all been through it; some more than once, and many with newly acquired insight into this turbulent life event.

Other books on the subject, no matter how expert their authors, are generally limited to the knowledge of only one person. Instead, we have assembled the experiences of hundreds of divorced people who have survived loneliness, anger, sadness, and pain, and emerged with wisdom to share. If two heads are better than one, as the saying goes, then hundreds of heads are even better.

As you might expect, we heard opposing views on some topics: For every person who vows to never speak to his or her ex-spouse again, there's a person equally dedicated to maintaining a friendship. Our goal was to present both views and let you choose for yourself.

Above all, we think you'll find that these survivor's stories—whether funny, furious, full of triumph or regret—illuminate the experience so many of us have shared or will share in the course of our lives.

JENNIFER BRIGHT REICH

KEY

So you'll know just how expert our respondents really are, we've included their credentials in this book. Look for these icons:

♥ = Married   Y = Years
♂ = Engaged   M = Months
💔 = Divorced

The Sharpest Thorn: Making the Decision to Divorce

Y*ou and your spouse are at a crossroads. Something's gotta give, and you already gave your sanity. What was once unthinkable—divorce from the person you once loved like no other— might be your only option. How can you be sure? Only your heart knows the truth. Read on to find out how others knew it was time to leave their love, and their marriage, behind.*

TRUST YOUR GUT. Don't stay in a marriage that you know is flawed because you think it will get better. Somewhere deep inside is a voice that is telling you to get out: Listen to that voice.

　　—ANONYMOUS
　　EAST PALESTINE, OHIO
　　💔4Y 💔13Y

DECIDING TO GET A DIVORCE IS LIKE CHOOSING THE BEST TIME FOR ROOT CANAL.

　　—KARIN TARPLEY
　　SEATTLE, WASHINGTON
　　💔4Y 💔5Y

MY HUSBAND WAS CARRYING ON an affair, and I simply could not live with the situation as it existed. I was in such acute pain that it was like a medical decision—if you have an infected arm that's not getting better, at some point you amputate the arm in order to survive.

—*ANONYMOUS*
GREENWICH, CONNECTICUT
45Y 1Y

• • • • • • • •

IT'S A PROCESS. The decision doesn't just come; it evolves. It usually takes a major event to fully recognize the marriage isn't working. When my wife told me she thought we should separate, it was really traumatic because it made me see that it was what I wanted to do all along, but I'd been too chicken to say it.

—*TIM GETZOFF*
BOULDER, COLORADO
5Y 4Y

• • • • • • • •

TRUST YOUR INTUITION. We were at his family's house taking our Christmas picture and something deep inside told me I'd better get a picture of everybody because I wouldn't be coming back next year. We divorced a year later.

—*LUCIA BOLES*
ST. LOUIS, MISSOURI
19Y 34Y

• • • • • • • •

WHEN YOUR SPOUSE SAYS he or she wants a divorce, do not believe the first story you get about why. It is such a monumental change that initial explanations or reasons are never the truth or real motivation for such a change.

—*NOAH SHUSSETT*
BROOKLYN, NEW YORK
14Y 3Y

If you know in your heart it's going to end, get out early before you become attached to old hurts and old possessions.

—*B.L.*
KIRKLAND,
WASHINGTON
22Y

DO IT YOUNG, before there are kids to complicate the issue. Recognize that you've grown away from the person you married when you were young and foolish.

> —*D.M.*
> *IOWA CITY, IOWA*
> 💔20Y 💔25Y

· · · · · · · ·

❝ My sister and her husband had to literally come to my house, take me in the car, and drive me to the divorce lawyer's office. That's how I started the proceedings. ❞

> —*FRANK*
> *CHARLESTON, SOUTH CAROLINA*
> 💔8Y 💔 💔38Y

· · · · · · · ·

HE CALLED ME ON THE PHONE and asked if I missed him. He had been in Guatemala for four months, and I realized that I didn't miss a lot of the things one would normally miss when a partner was gone. We simply didn't share them any longer, and hadn't for a long time. My life was easier, more peaceful, and more fun without him around, and although I was brought up to believe that marriage should be forever, the thought of living with this person the rest of my life was depressing.

> —*JOANNE WOLFE*
> *NESKOWIN, OREGON*
> 💔8Y 💔2Y

DIVORCE DATA

The first recorded divorce in American history occurred in a Massachusetts Puritan court in 1639.

HEADLINES
Best Advice and Top Tips

- Trust your instincts. If you think your marriage is making you unhappy, it is.

- Seek counsel from family, friends, and clergy. Imagine what life with your current spouse will look like in the future.

- Learn to put your wants and needs first.

- No matter how scary it is being on your own, it's better to be by yourself than to be lonely with someone else.

You can have doubts and have bad times, but when it's over you cannot deny it. You know; your heart just won't let you try anymore.

—PETER STEUR
BRISBANE,
AUSTRALIA
💔6Y 💔 💔4Y
💔2Y

IF YOUR WIFE IS BOLD ENOUGH to tell you she's going to be unfaithful, believe her. My ex-wife told me that one day she was going to cheat on me. It was in the heat of an argument. I didn't want to believe it, but it happened. We were moving to a new city, and she moved a month before me to establish our home. I stayed to finish out my job, and when I arrived, she'd shacked up with another guy only a block away from our new home.

—ANONYMOUS
SYRACUSE, NEW
YORK
💔7Y

KNOW THAT SOMETIMES it's the right thing to do. No one gets married wanting to get divorced. But sometimes you simply outgrow a marriage, and the best thing is to part amicably. It's helpful for people to know that divorce can sometimes be the best thing for both people, or at least, best for one person and the best thing that the other one can give them.

> —*JEAN NICK*
> *KINTNERSVILLE, PENNSYLVANIA*
> 💔 *13Y SEPARATED 4Y*

• • • • • • • •

I WAS ON VACATION with my husband, and what each of us wanted to see and do was so different. On this trip I realized that what we valued, appreciated, and embraced were quite different.

> —*ANONYMOUS*
> *SAN FRANCISCO, CALIFORNIA*
> 💔 *5Y* 💔 *1Y*

• • • • • • • •

I REALIZED I WAS A SERVANT hoping for appreciation. I married needing love: There was little to none of it at home growing up. My husband was an excessive drinker and abusive. I lost all of my friends and became submissive. A divorce was the only answer: The alternative was to spend another 30 years in misery.

> —*ANONYMOUS*
> 💔 *22Y*

• • • • • • • •

MY FIRST WIFE THREATENED ME with divorce every time she got mad at me. It finally stopped when I beat her to the punch. If you think a divorce is coming, make the first move. There are many advantages to filing the papers yourself instead of waiting for your rotten spouse to do it.

> —*S.J.*
> *ZELIENOPLE, PENNSYLVANIA*
> 💔 *5Y* 💔 *13Y*

MY HUSBAND WAS SPENDING less time at home and was less affectionate. Sometimes he would give me a creepy look—almost an "I hate you" look. One time he had this expression on his face. I said, "What's wrong?" He said, "Were I to tell you, it would just hurt your feelings." When it gets like that, it's time to start mentally preparing for what's coming: You need to start forming a plan.

—*JENNIFER*
LAS VEGAS, NEVADA
8Y ♥ 20Y

• • • • • • • •

" One day you just wake up and say, 'I made a big mistake. I'm out of here.' My advice? Do it. Don't overthink it. "

—*EILEEN*
WEST STOCKBRIDGE, MASSACHUSETTS

• • • • • • • •

MY HUSBAND SAID TO ME, "It hurts me too much to be nice to you. Being nice to you isn't in my best interest." Well, the only decision I had left to make after that was who gets the house.

—*TARY PARIS*
LINCOLN, NEBRASKA
5Y ♥ 10Y

• • • • • • • •

A LIGHT WENT ON FOR ME when my father said, "I'd rather see my daughter happily divorced than unhappily married." I knew he was right, and I filed for divorce shortly after.

—*ROBIN VELLIS*
CLARKS SUMMIT, PENNSYLVANIA
1Y ♥ 4Y

KNOW YOUR ENEMIES

One of my wife's friends came up to me out of the blue one day and said, "I probably shouldn't be telling you this, but if you show up tomorrow at the bowling alley at five o'clock, you might see somebody leaving with someone else." So I went, and sure enough, there was my wife with this random guy, getting into a taxi together. Furious, I followed them across town to his house and waited in my car while they went inside together. After five minutes, I got out and knocked on the front door. I heard scrambling and tumbling, so obviously something had been going on. Then the guy called out, "Who are you?" My reply: "I'm the husband of the woman in your bed—come out here on the street." He stayed behind a locked door; I could see my wife peering out at me from behind the curtains. This is probably a good thing, because it gave me time to calm down and reevaluate my priorities. Beforehand, I had been ready to kill the guy. Once I calmed down, I realized he wasn't worth going to jail for.

Instead, my wife and I divorced, and I learned an important lesson in the process: Be careful whom you share your secrets with. The woman who told on my wife had started out hating me because she and my wife would always male-bash together. Eventually, however, as she saw how hard I was working to keep our failing marriage together for the sake of the children, she began secretly feeling sympathy for me. After a while, the guilt started eating her alive, so she spilled my wife's secret. That woman is my new wife today.

—*KERRY MCINTOSH*
CASTLE ROCK, COLORADO
3Y 💔 22Y

DIVORCE DATA

By the late 1700s, divorce was common enough in America that scholars were criticizing "the high divorce rates."

FOR THE CATHOLICS OUT THERE: Talk to your priest and ask for the papers to begin the annulment process. It's a huge document in which you are asked to give a summary of your and your ex's lives and relationships. If anything, the annulment process will make you painfully analyze each and every step of your relationship to understand what went wrong. This process is tedious, gut-wrenching, and forces a person to analyze her behavior. I learned a lot about myself and how I can make my relationships better and mutually satisfying.

—*D.L.*
CHICAGO, ILLINOIS
❤6Y ❤5Y

• • • • • • • • •

ASK YOUR CLOSEST FAMILY and friends, whose opinions you value, what they think about your spouse and the situation. Sometimes when you are in the throes of problems with someone you love, it is difficult to really see what is going on. Getting an outside opinion from those who know you best can help you make a decision.

—*DAWN PETCHELL*
ARLINGTON, VIRGINIA
❤2Y ❤1Y

• • • • • • • • •

 NO MATTER HOW MUCH in love you think you are, or that you've really found the right person, you should not get married at 18. At that age, you're still trying to figure out who you are and what you want out of life. It's way too early to get hitched. I married too young the first time, and I'm still paying for it. Now I have to live with the fact that I was part of a failed marriage.

—*KEVIN L.*
PITTSBURGH, PENNSYLVANIA
❤9Y ❤14Y

I GRADUALLY CAME TO THE REALIZATION that I couldn't live with somebody *all the time.* I never stopped loving my wife, or missing her when we were apart, but I couldn't be with her day in and day out. The hardest parts were telling my wife how I felt and having to explain to my friends why I was leaving the marriage. Some people just didn't get it. But I had to be truthful with myself and honest with the people I loved. As a result, my ex-wife and I are still very close, and we still spend time together.

—*M.W.E.*
LINCOLN CITY, OREGON
🕊19Y 💔 🕊8Y

No one else can tell you to leave until you are ready to go. My success was not going back once I left.

—*BARBARA*
KETCHIKAN,
ALASKA
🕊 💔16Y

THE TRUTH HURTS

When I first confronted my husband about rumors that he had been cheating, he said, "It happened one time months ago. I realized I love you and want to work it out." I gave him the benefit of the doubt and tried getting past it. One day I tried to call him at work, but he was at the company Christmas party. I decided to go there. I walked in and saw him with his arm around another woman. That's when I realized I had been lied to, manipulated, and played for a fool, and I knew it was time to let him go. I looked him in the eye and asked, "How could you do this to me?" He answered, "Because I'm not happy anymore."

When I walked out of that building, I had a bad panic attack: I couldn't breathe, I couldn't stand, I thought I was dying. I decided I would never allow another person to make me feel like that again.

—*JENNIFER W.*
GREENVILLE, MISSOURI
🕊12Y 💔1Y

DIVORCE DATA

The state with the highest divorce rate is Nevada.

THE MOST DIFFICULT ASPECT is coming to the realization that regardless of how much I loved him, or how badly I wanted to work it out, it didn't matter to him. He didn't feel the same way. When one wants out and the other doesn't, it's a terrible slap in the face.

—*STELLA SHANANAQUET*
  ADRIAN, MICHIGAN
  ❤1Y 💔PENDING

· · · · · · · · ·

DON'T LET YOUR MARRIAGE take a backseat to other interests or priorities. A marriage takes constant work and tenderness. After 22 years of marriage, my husband decided to have an affair with his secretary. I filed for divorce after I found out.

—*NANCY*
  TAMPA, FLORIDA
  ❤ 💔 ❤

SEEKING INNER PEACE

I left four times, and I always came back. My in-laws at the time told me, "God will never forgive you if you leave," and, my favorite, "You will burn in hell if you get divorced." So I went looking for answers in church and, thankfully, I got them. My priest told me that the church always encouraged you to work things out, but that people who did not love each other should part ways. I asked him, "How do you know when to leave for good?" I remember him saying, "It's just an inner peace you feel." Back then, I thought he was nuts: inner peace? But honestly, there was a point in my life—about a year after seeing the priest—when I woke up with a new confidence in myself and what I felt my life could be like if I were on my own. I left that day and never came back.

—*L.M.*
  CHICAGO, ILLINOIS

SOMETIMES IT HELPS TO THINK about where your life is going. I was married for more than 23 years. Most of that time, my husband and I didn't speak to each other. We simply led separate lives, like roommates. At least we didn't fight! But at one point I thought to myself, do I want to be 50 years old, still living like this? That's when I decided to get divorced.

> —L.G.K.
> EASTON, PENNSYLVANIA
> ♥23Y ♥5Y

. . . .

❝ I knew that it was time to make a move the day I realized that I was crying more than I was laughing. ❞

> —SAMANTHA
> LOS ANGELES, CALIFORNIA
> ♥2Y ♥4Y

. . . .

YOU KNOW IT IS TIME to separate when you wake up and realize you are not happy; you just want to go to work and you dread coming home to your spouse. Simple communication becomes difficult. Your ability to be intimate does not exist, and you are left in a void. You realize that you *have* to move on or you will die inside. You go through many phases—realization, fear, and acceptance, and, in my case, the mutual decision that it's time to move on.

> —RICH SCHAFLER
> NEW YORK, NEW YORK
> ♥ ♥

DIVORCE DATA

The state with the lowest divorce rate is Massachusetts.

Do what is right for *you!* No one else will. There's no excuse for staying in a relationship that isn't healthy.

—*CELIA DUNBAR*
OKLAHOMA CITY,
OKLAHOMA
💔20Y 💔4Y

YOU HAVE TO BE BRUTALLY HONEST with each other. If you're not, it leaves a little glimmer of hope in your heart that things might be OK. Honesty may hurt, but it's much better than dragging things on. For me it was over when my wife said, "You've become more like a friend than a lover. I don't think I can have sex with you anymore." Hearing that hurt. But there was nothing I could do except take it like a man and move on.

—*JOHN COOKE*
GREELEY, COLORADO
💔20Y 💔2Y

• • • • • • • •

I REMEMBER TALKING TO A FRIEND of mine before I had decided my marriage was over, and she told me that when I knew it was over I wouldn't have to question it because there would be nothing I could do about it. She was right. When my wife and I did decide that the point had come, we both just cried and held each other. It was kind of beautiful, actually—sad, but beautiful.

—*PETER STEUR*
BRISBANE, AUSTRALIA
💔6Y 💔 💔4Y 💔2Y

• • • • • • • •

IF YOUR SPOUSE IS A VIOLENT PERSON and has shown it on more than one occasion, there is only one thing you should do: Get out. Don't try to rationalize or help him or counsel him or tell yourself that you are somehow to blame. If he is abusive, leave immediately. I stayed long enough to get a broken arm that never healed right.

—*G.P.*
POLAND, OHIO
💔2Y 💔 💔2M

My husband made the decision. I asked offhandedly after an argument if we should really be together and he said, "No." That may not have been the best approach for him to take, but I really don't know what approach would have been better. At first I was annoyed at his timing because it was right before a retreat with my writing group, and I knew I wouldn't get done all the writing I'd planned. But it turned out to be the best thing possible—to have a weekend surrounded by supportive, caring, wise women of all ranks and ages, in a beautiful, natural environment—I came home much stronger for it.

> —*Karin Tarpley*
> *Seattle, Washington*
> 💔4y 💔5y

THERE ARE SIGNS EVERYWHERE

There were a million positive reasons not to leave: My garden, my cats, dear friends, good work. However, my relationship had become so deeply nightmarish I could not find any resolution or direction. One day I was driving in downtown Los Angeles and saw a huge sign: U-Haul. That's it! It's that simple! U-Haul was the answer! I could simply haul out and be free. I drove into the parking lot, walked into the office, and bought 60 boxes, all the same size. I took the boxes home, and after folding and packing my first one I knew I was going to be OK. I had no plan, no place to go as of yet, but, I was filling boxes: something was finally happening. Momentum!

> —*Hawley Hussey*
> *Brooklyn, New York*
> 💔 💔2y

I KNEW MY MARRIAGE WAS OVER WHEN . . .

. . . WE STARTED MARRIAGE COUNSELING. I wanted to keep going, and he didn't want to go anymore. If he wasn't willing to try, what hope was there?

> —C.B.
> *ATLANTA, GEORGIA*
> 🌼1Y 💔16Y

• • • • • • • •

. . . ONE DAY I WAS SCRUBBING the dining room chairs, and I thought, "Is this all there is?" I knew then, sure as anything, that there was more. Betty Friedan told me: That's when I knew it was over.

> —*SHARON LONDON*
> *SAN FRANCISCO, CALIFORNIA*
> 🌼16Y 💔29Y

• • • • • • • •

. . . I REALIZED I HAD NEVER BEEN ABLE to be my own person, and this was something I suddenly wanted desperately—to be myself.

> —*MONICA WILLETT*
> *FORT MYERS, FLORIDA*
> 🌼12Y 💔1M

• • • • • • • •

. . . MY DAUGHTER TOLD ME about daddy's girl-friend, who he had in our house, and who had stolen most of my clothes (including my undergarments).

> —B.D.
> *STUTTGART, GERMANY*
> 🌼7Y 💔4Y

• • • • • • • •

. . . HE FIRST HIT ME. But it took me three years of counseling and denial to get me out of it.

> —R.F.
> *TEL AVIV, ISRAEL*
> 🌼9Y 💔4Y

. . . I REALIZED SHE ALREADY HAD a replacement for me.

—*DAVID LODGE*
OKLAHOMA CITY, OKLAHOMA
❤6Y 💔1Y

• • • • • • • •

. . . THE LAST 10 COWS (down from 100) were sold on our farm, and the fields and barns were empty.

—*LINDA*
FALMOUTH, MAINE
❤30Y 💔1Y

• • • • • • • •

I FOUND OUT MY HUSBAND was having an affair. You never want to believe it's true, but after a little sneaking around I managed to drum up the evidence I needed to get him to admit it. That was the end of a 17-year marriage—just like that!

—*F.R.*
SYDNEY, AUSTRALIA
❤17Y 💔2Y

• • • • • • • •

ON OUR EIGHTH ANNIVERSARY, my husband came home from work drunk. He took me out for pizza, then dropped me off at home before going out with his friends. As I watched *Dukes of Hazzard,* I realized that there wouldn't be a ninth anniversary. I left ten days later.

—*DIANE EVANS*
RENTON, WASHINGTON
❤8Y 💔 ❤6Y 💔 ❤13Y

• • • • • • • •

. . . I FOUND MYSELF DAYDREAMING of someone coming to inform me of the tragic news that my husband had been killed in a car accident or killed in a disaster on his job site or killed in any other various ways (you get the idea).

—*JAMIE TEAL*
NATICK, MASSACHUSETTS
❤3Y 💔 ❤3Y

. . . A MAN KISSED ME and made me realize how unhappy I was.

> —A.P.
> CHAPEL HILL, NORTH CAROLINA
> 3Y 2Y

. . . A CHEAP LOCAL HOTEL showed up on our bank statement. He was diagnosed with genital herpes that same week. I was able to survive by taking my own unfortunate situation and subsequent infection with herpes and turning it into a full-blown STD patient advocacy program. I found a way to help others, and this empowered me. Currently I am the Lead Patient Advocate for Valtrex and speak around the United States on the risks, preventions, and treatments of STDs.

> —GAYLA MCCORD
> SHIRLEY, INDIANA
> 5Y 1Y

. . . WE HAD BEEN HAVING some problems, and I asked my husband point-blank if he loved me. His response was, "I don't know," to which I asked him, "Don't you think that's a problem?"

> —FRAN WILLS
> LITTLETON, COLORADO
> 7Y 5Y

. . . I REALIZED THAT WE WERE living separate lives. It hit me one Christmas when my husband attended a party at his real estate office, but he didn't even tell me about it. I only learned about it the next day when I saw the invitation!

> —M.S.L.
> WAIKOLOA, HAWAII
> 37Y 3Y

. . . HE WANTED TO SIT in his chair in front of the TV for the rest of his life, and I knew that wasn't going to do it for me.

> —GRACE
> CHAPEL HILL, NORTH CAROLINA
> 22Y 31Y

. . . DURING THE LAST SIX MONTHS of my marriage, my wife was addicted to online chat rooms. She'd come home from work and log in and still be online at 4 a.m.

> —*W.N.*
> *DOUGLASVILLE, GEORGIA*
> 18Y 11Y 7Y

- - - - - - - -

. . . I REALIZED MY FIRST WIFE and I made good friends and even good roommates, but had very different visions of the kind of life we wanted to live.

> —*STEVE*
> *HOLLYWOOD, CALIFORNIA*

- - - - - - - -

. . . I WOKE UP ONE DAY and said, "This is the day."

> —*EVE CARTWRIGHT*
> *NEEDHAM, MASSACHUSETTS*
> 5Y 7Y

- - - - - - - -

. . . I WAS EATING BREAKFAST of strawberries, bananas, yogurt, and wheat germ, and my wife came into the room after a week of doing things like staying out all night. She sat down, looked at me and at the food I was eating, and said, "You're not really going to eat that shit, are you?" I looked at her and said, "That's it, it's over."

> —*DAVID FEDER*
> *DES MOINES, IOWA*
> 5Y 8Y

- - - - - - - -

. . . MY HUSBAND SHOWED absolutely no interest in becoming a father. I was already pregnant and excited about having the baby. But he was indifferent at best, hostile at worst. We were only married for ten months. I decided it was better to raise the baby alone than in a hostile, unhappy home.

> —*ANONYMOUS*
> *VALLEJO, CALIFORNIA*
> 35Y

I REALIZED MY HUSBAND really didn't want our marriage to survive. When I saw that I was fourth on his list (behind his parents, work, and baseball), I also realized I was too far down the list to bother wanting to be on it. Only then did I want to be free of that man. As moments go, it was actually kind of joyful. I remember leaving the counselor's office, driving over the Golden Gate Bridge and feeling so free.

—*BONNIE RUSSELL*
DEL MAR, CALIFORNIA
4Y 4Y

· · · · · · · · ·

" There are a whole lot of things worse than being lonely. Living with someone who demeans you, lies to you, or betrays you is worse than being lonely. "

—*M.L.E.*
SARATOGA SPRINGS, NEW YORK
12Y 5Y

· · · · · · · · ·

MY WIFE HAD AN AFFAIR with my good friend and co-worker. I found out and I restrained myself from beating the hell out of him, which I deeply regret. Ultimately, you have to remember it's all for the best: divorce was the right thing. As far as how to get through it, I drank a lot—frequently and in large quantities.

—*EVAN*
ATLANTA, GEORGIA
1Y 5Y

HEARD IT THROUGH THE GRAPEVINE

I should have known better than to get married in the first place. Things had always been kind of rocky from the start. I was a struggling trader on the Mercantile Exchange in Chicago and had a tough time making ends meet; she was doing well working for a drug company. She always made a point to let me know how well she did; she rubbed it in my face. She used to tell me that trading wasn't a real job and since I had been on the trading floor for so long I really had no other job skills.

One day, she told me she had a conference she had to attend downtown and I remember telling her that she looked nice in the outfit she was wearing. As I found out later, she spent the day downtown with her VP of Marketing, who was also married and who had two children. There was no conference.

As fate had it, Chicago turned out to be a pretty small city that day. I got a couple of phone calls from some guys I knew who insisted they saw my wife holding hands with a man downtown. I did not believe them, but I was still disturbed by the information. I asked my wife, and she immediately dismissed the news as non-sense. I told the guys over dinner that they were mistaken, but I could tell by the look in their eyes that I had been lied to by my wife. They even described the outfit I had compli-mented her on. I asked my wife again the next day, and she denied the allegation. I kept asking until she finally broke down and told me it was none of my business and that she didn't have to tell me anything. Needless to say, from that moment on I realized I had a problem.

—ANONYMOUS
CHICAGO, ILLINOIS

MY WIFE ACTED LIKE EVERYTHING she desired was important, and everything I wanted wasn't. My job means the world to me, and she started begging me to stay home during the days and be with her. At the same time, when I came home at night, she insisted on going out and partying with her friends without me. It was always about what she wanted, all of the time.

—*STEVEN GREEN*
LOS ANGELES, CALIFORNIA
🖤10Y 💔19Y

CROSSING THE FINISH LINE

My father was going through his second bone marrow transplant, and my mother had been diagnosed with liver cancer and had months to live. I needed a break from the pressure so I spent a lot of time running. A goal of mine was to run the Chicago Marathon. I told my wife I was going to run it and that it would mean a lot if she came out to see me. She went to Vegas instead with her friends. While I was running, I thought a lot. It was a very emotional run for me. I never felt so alone; both my parents ill, brothers and sisters living out of state, and a wife who simply did not care. I finished the marathon and ran into the reception area where family members and significant others waited. There was no one there for me, and I suddenly felt empowered. I thought to myself, "If this is marriage, I don't want it." I limped five miles back to my car. I was gone when my wife came home from Vegas.

—*ADAM*
CHICAGO, ILLINOIS

WE WERE SITTING ON A PARK BENCH, watching a Little League game, when I just said, "It's over, and I want you to leave."

—*SARAH*
SEATTLE, WASHINGTON
💔5Y 💔4Y

· · · · · · · · ·

I REALIZED THAT I'D RATHER BE DIVORCED and feel lonely than be married and still feel alone all the time.

—*A.P.*
BOARDMAN, OHIO
💔12Y 💔 💔14Y

· · · · · · · · ·

DIVORCE DATA

Smokers are more likely than non-smokers to be divorced: 49 percent versus 32 percent.

IF YOU ARE CONSIDERING a divorce, you've already made the decision. It's not something you think about unless there is very good reason. Don't try to find reasons *not* to do it.

—*BRITTANY MELLOR*
ZELIENOPLE, PENNSYLVANIA
💔5Y 💔2Y

· · · · · · · · ·

ASK THESE QUESTIONS and see where you land:
1. Will I enjoy being with this woman the rest of my life?
2. Does she make me feel good?
3. Does she satisfy me?
4. Does it get any better?
5. Is it right for me?
6. Why am I thinking about leaving?

—*JIM HOLLAND*
WASHINGTON, D.C.
💔6Y 💔 💔5Y 💔1Y

I knew that my marriage was over when I couldn't stand to hold his hand anymore. It made my skin crawl.

—SAMANTHA
  LOS ANGELES,
  CALIFORNIA
  2Y 4Y

I WAS ON A TRIP to Washington, D.C., and I realized that I was the same age my father had been the last time we were both in D.C., and he had died on that trip. I was doing the same things my father did on the last day of his life, and I thought, "I'm that age now; I could die tonight. Am I happy? No. And I need to be happy." It was an epiphany. I came home from that trip and decided to make some changes.

—SHELLEY
  DES MOINES, IOWA
  8Y 5Y

- - - - - - - -

IS YOUR HEART HEAVY? Gather as much information from your friends and family as you can, and then take some quiet time for yourself. Just sit, be quiet, and listen to what your heart tells you. Your heart knows what is right for you.

—DAWN PETCHELL
  ARLINGTON, VIRGINIA
  2Y 1Y

- - - - - - - -

THINK OF THE ALTERNATIVE! If you don't get a divorce, it means you want back in the old marriage. You haven't any choice. A divorce can be a great liberation. It's a time to make new (and better) choices. It's positive. The marriage was the negative.

—CHRISTINE EMMERT
  VALLEY FORGE, PENNSYLVANIA
  4Y 32Y

- - - - - - - -

THERE IS ONE KEY TRUTH I eventually (and belatedly) grasped during a counseling session: The counselor said, "When the words and the actions don't match, the truth is in the action."

—BONNIE RUSSELL
  DEL MAR, CALIFORNIA
  4Y 4Y

FINDING OUT THE HARD WAY

When e-mail was very new, we had a home account that I hadn't used before. I asked my husband to log me on so I could send some e-mails. He did, and then he went to bed.

In the course of sending e-mails, I came across pictures that my husband had sent to another man. He had been corresponding regularly with him, and it was headed in a romantic direction. I was afraid to confront him, because I knew he wouldn't react well: He came from a very prominent family, and it would not be accepted.

So I made a panicked phone call to my friend in the middle of the night. I didn't know what to do. She told me to save the e-mails on a disk. In the morning, when my husband woke, he was hugging me and asking me what was wrong. He could tell by the way I was acting that something was on my mind. But then he went to work. I called him, got his voice mail, and told him that I was leaving, and I didn't say why. I got out of there and stayed with a friend that night. That's when I finally told him what I had found; he completely denied it.

I knew we couldn't go to counseling and work it out, although he wanted to try. I said, "You sent him pictures of yourself on our honeymoon, and some guy sent a naked picture of himself to you. This just isn't something we can work out."

—*ANONYMOUS*
ATLANTA, GEORGIA
3Y 8Y

WALKING ON WATER . . . AND OUT THE DOOR

After a few years of marriage, my second husband started spending a great deal of time with his attorney. They took business trips together, and she called him every night after supper. One night, I cooked a special dinner hoping to improve things in my marriage. My husband said to me, "You'll never guess what Anita said today."

I said, "No, dear, what did she say?"

My husband said, "She told me that I have no idea how important I am. When I walk through the parking lot at work, the staff is thrilled to brush the cloth on my jacket."

I said, "And how did you respond?"

He said, "I told her she was right! I had no idea that I was that important!"

That was when I knew my goose was cooked. There was no way I could muster up enough baloney to make my husband think he could walk on water like that. Our marriage ended not too long after that.

> —*Rosanna*
> *New York, New York*
> *21y*

Heartbreak Hotel: The First Stage of Separation

*T*he clothes have been packed, the new residence has been established, and it's official: You're no longer a couple. Now comes
the hardest part. If you're serious about getting a divorce and start-
ing a new life, you've got to get through the first stage of separation.
As you'll read in this chapter, it's no picnic. But with some good
advice and a little help from your friends, you'll make it through.

WHEN DEALING WITH LONELINESS, remember all
the things that annoyed you about your ex, like
picking up his shoes or doing his laundry. Think
about them daily.

—*ANONYMOUS*
SAN ANTONIO, TEXAS
💔3Y 💔6M

**CRY UNTIL IT'S
DONE. THIS COULD
TAKE MONTHS.**

—*HAWLEY HUSSEY*
*BROOKLYN,
NEW YORK*
💔 💔2Y

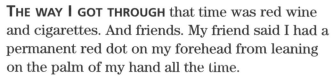

THE WAY I GOT THROUGH that time was red wine and cigarettes. And friends. My friend said I had a permanent red dot on my forehead from leaning on the palm of my hand all the time.

—*ANONYMOUS*
ATLANTA, GEORGIA
💔3Y 💔8Y

• • • • • • • •

The worst thing about being divorced is the time immediately after.

—*BONNIE LAMB*
CHICAGO, ILLINOIS
💔15Y 💔13Y

I FOUND SUPPORT through three friends— especially my friend Yolanda. I could call her all hours of the night. No matter how tired Yolanda was, she would always listen to me babble on the phone. Now, that's a good friend!

—*KY'A JACKSON*
PHILADELPHIA, PENNSYLVANIA
💔1Y 💔5Y

• • • • • • • •

EVEN THOUGH MY MARRIAGE was over for several years before I left the property, my home was hard to leave because I had put so much into it. So I put a lot of effort into our new residence, even if it was only a rental. The kids' input was of great importance to me. I wanted them to feel they had some control over their new home.

—*TRACY*
FREDERICK, MARYLAND
💔15Y 💔1Y

• • • • • • • •

I NEEDED TO FIND a temporary place to live, but we were in another country and I didn't know a lot of people, nor did I have much money. I pretended I was single and on my own, and it just wasn't working out with my two male roommates (one was my husband). I also kept the location of my new digs a secret from my husband for about two months, because I was frightened of his behavior.

—*KIM*
MINNEAPOLIS, MINNESOTA
💔4Y 💔4Y

WHEN I LEFT MY MARRIAGE, I also left the house. I found a temporary apartment on the grounds of a local college campus for the summer. This was a place where I felt safe, and where I was surrounded by beauty and nature. I spent a lot of time outside, just walking, feeding the ducks in the pond near the house, and trying to heal. When I think of trying to get to know myself as a single woman again, I think of the months I spent in that little apartment.

   —*PAMELA*
      PHILADELPHIA, PENNSYLVANIA
      18Y 15Y

❝Take time to process your marriage—what was right, what went wrong. And, give yourself that time to heal. Forgive yourself, cry, get angry, whatever it takes.❞

   —*DAWN PETCHELL*
      ARLINGTON, VIRGINIA
      2Y 1Y

AFTER I THREW HIM OUT, I found out he was staying in a seedy motel: That made me happy. Then, I later found out he got lice from the pillow in the seedy motel: That made me even happier. If you are going to kick your spouse out, make him as uncomfortable as possible.

   —*R.D.*
      KEEZLETOWN, VIRGINIA
      13Y 18Y

HEAD LINES
Best Advice and Top Tips

- Lean on your friends; they will help you through the hard times.
- Let yourself cry as much as you need to—and then get over it.
- If possible, change your surroundings as much as you can— new house, new city, new state.
- Think about your life before you were married.
- Approach divorce as a chance to make a new start.

PUT SOME MONEY AWAY, or keep a credit card with a good chunk of unused credit, so you are prepared for any unexpected changes that might occur. My husband and I continued living together after he decided we were getting a divorce: He thought he should be able to remain in our home, with me and the children, and also spend weekends with his girlfriend. Looking back, I can see that the children and I would have been better off staying somewhere else, but I did not have the financial resources to move us.

—*MARGARET*
BOULDER, COLORADO
💔13Y 💔14Y

• • • • • • • •

MY GIRLFRIENDS WANTED TO take me out and drown my sorrows with alcohol, which did work to a certain degree. At least it enabled me to forget the whole thing for a little while. But eventually I had to sober up.

—*M.K.M.*
OWINGS, MARYLAND
💔2Y 💔1Y

IT WAS A REAL AWAKENING to be alone. I rented a small studio apartment. I connected with a couple of the other single women in the building. One night a week, we would get together at one of our apartments or go out for dinner. It was good to have the company. It made me realize that it hadn't been healthy for me or my ex-husband to spend all of our free time together.

—*M.G.*
    BELLEVILLE, ILLINOIS
    3Y 1Y

I GOT OUT OF DODGE. I've been divorced twice now: In each case, I didn't want to remain in the same town, where I could run into him or see him with another woman. I left my first husband in Los Angeles and moved with the kids to San Francisco. I left my second husband in San Francisco and moved to Boston!

—*MAGGIE*
    BROOKLINE, MASSACHUSETTS
    5Y 2Y 2Y

NO MATTER THE CIRCUMSTANCES around a divorce, you will feel hurt and pain. Just remember that the sadness you feel now will fade over time.

—*D.N.*
    EUREKA SPRINGS, ARKANSAS
    4Y

BE GRACIOUS WHEN people ask the inevitable: "Why are you getting divorced?" Avoid saying anything negative about your soon-to-be-ex and simply say, "It didn't work out." Leave out the gory details and maintain your dignity.

—*JIM*
    ELIZABETHTOWN, KENTUCKY
    33Y

A LITTLE LESS HAPPY

In 1973, 67.4 percent of couples rated their marriages as "very happy," but in 1996 that number dropped to 61.9 percent.

THE FIRST TIME I GOT DIVORCED, we slept in separate rooms for three months. That was not in the best interest of anyone. I finally moved to a new city for work, and she stayed behind. But the second time I got divorced, I came home and my wife was waiting for me on the porch with my suitcase. I picked it up and hauled ass: I was never so glad to be out of a place.

—ANONYMOUS
SIKESTON, MISSOURI
💔15Y 💔 💔6Y 💔

. . . .

" A divorce is like a death. You go through the grieving process, mourning over the fact that a marriage has died. "

—B.E.A.
BLAN, OHIO
💔7Y 💔8Y

. . . .

INITIALLY YOU ARE COMPLETELY OVERWHELMED and don't think you will survive. But you can, with some help. My mother is a supreme optimist; she's not always realistic, but she's always positive. We would sit up at night at 2 a.m. or 3 a.m. drinking tea. That's the Australian/English cure for anything: the cup of tea. We would just talk through it and cry through it. Wine and vodka tonics were pretty helpful at times, too.

—F.R.
SYDNEY, AUSTRALIA
💔17Y 💔2Y

THE ONE THING THAT COULD HAVE KEPT YOU MARRIED

DRUGS. Either for me or for her. But with both of us sober it was never going to work.

> —*FELIX DELERME*
> *GREENFORD, OHIO*
> 7Y 2Y

. . . .

HONESTY. He had a drinking problem but he just wouldn't face up to it. He lied to me about his drinking over and over, but worse than that, he lied to himself. If he would have just been willing to face the problem, I would have been there to support him all the way. But he kept hiding his head in the sand. You just can't help someone who doesn't want to be helped and doesn't think they need help. So I left.

> —*E.C.*
> *WINONA, OHIO*
> 10Y 5Y 15Y

. . . .

IF MY EX GOT OFF HIS BUTT and did something with himself, I could've stayed. Also, if he hadn't pushed me away when I got a place of my own, it may have worked. I just wanted my space, and from that moment he's been a total jerk. It's his loss; I have much better things in my life now.

> —*H.O.*
> *EVERETT, WASHINGTON*
> 2Y 1Y 1Y

. . . .

IF HE HAD REALLY LOVED ME, instead of deceiving me, that would have kept me married to him . . . but he was unfaithful from the get-go and we should never have gotten married.

> —*S.G.*
> *CARSON CITY, NEVADA*
> 4Y 8Y

ON THE FIRST DAY BY YOURSELF, you go through an emotional rollercoaster. You savor your newfound freedom, but soon come to the scary realization that you are now alone. I got through it with the support of my parents and sisters, as well as my friends being on call whenever I needed them.

—*RICH SCHAFLER*
NEW YORK, NEW YORK

- - - - - - - -

A DIVORCE IS EASY if you own nothing and have no children. And, if it's an option, moving to another country also helps.

—*R.J.*
REDMOND, WASHINGTON
10Y 11Y

- - - - - - - -

ONE DAY I MET UP WITH an old college roommate who lived in a house with some friends, and after I confided to her how unhappy I was in my marriage, she suggested that I move in with them. When my husband was gone I packed my belongings, left him a note, and moved out. I had an instant community of people my own age. I was able to create a new life fairly quickly, and I started dating a friend of one of the guys in the house. If I had moved into an apartment by myself, I would have had a much more difficult time.

—*ELAINE*
SEATTLE, WASHINGTON
3Y 29Y

- - - - - - - -

PRAYER HELPS. Early on, I felt tremendous guilt regarding my child: The nights when he was with his dad were the worst. Finally, with time and a lot of prayer, I learned to not feel guilty.

—*SUZANNE*
FORT COLLINS, COLORADO

There's really no easy divorce. You go through a grieving period and eventually find yourself, and a new direction for your life.

—*D.M.*
LONG ISLAND,
NEW YORK
3Y 17Y

WHEN YOU'RE IN THE THROES OF A DIVORCE, it's way too easy to sit down and cry, and frankly, crying and being angry just make a person tired! I kept a journal of everything we went through. It was therapeutic for me to write about my fears and my failures, and let it go when I closed the cover of the book. It was easy to wake up the next day with a clean slate. I still read those journal entries every now and then. They keep things in perspective for me; I don't take anything for granted.

> —*LORI*
> *CHICAGO, ILLINOIS*

• • • • • • • •

" I decided I needed to just get over him, so I partied for two weeks. I'm a student, and it was during a break, so no harm, no foul. It did help. "

> —*STACEY*
> *DETROIT, MICHIGAN*

• • • • • • • •

I REFER TO THE TIME AFTER DIVORCE as the "accordion mourning process." For the first one to three months, you come in tight to your feelings, and you see very few people except close friends and counselors. Then, you slowly release and add more time out, and more people, until you are over the shock period.

> —*ANONYMOUS*
> *AMHERST, MASSACHUSETTS*

I'M SO LONELY, I COULD . . .

LONELINESS IS A STATE OF MIND. There is no getting around the fact that you are going to spend some time by yourself. If you dwell on it and make it a negative, you are allowing your ex to win. There is nothing wrong with spending some time by yourself, especially after a divorce. It's the perfect time to work through your feelings and allow yourself to move on. Don't avoid those free hours; embrace them. I was able to do much clearer thinking about my marriage and my life in those moments than I was ever able to do while I was still married. It enabled me to make sense out of what had happened and come to grips with it being a good thing for me. You really need some time by yourself.

> —R.M.
> BOARDMAN, OHIO
> 💔16Y 💔21Y

REACH OUT TO YOUR FAITH. Loneliness was a problem for me during my divorce. I was in a lonely marriage for 12 years before I got divorced. During my divorce, I felt separated from my family, too. I didn't even feel like I fit into my church anymore. But it was still a part of my life, and looking back I realize that it was my faith that pulled me through my divorce.

> —PENNY PHIPPS
> TUCSON, ARIZONA
> 💔12Y 💔 💔15Y

CONSIDER THAT LONELINESS can depend on age. When you are older, most of your friends are married, so you can't reach out to them all of the time; they have their own families and responsibilities. I found that joining support groups was very helpful, and they are a great place to meet new people. Through them, I could see the light at the end of the tunnel.

> —G.D.V.
> PRINCETON, NEW JERSEY
> 💔22Y 💔PENDING

GET OUT THERE, especially in the beginning. I joined a support group and made a lot of new friends. I started taking ballroom dance lessons and made more new friends. I volunteered for a special committee at my local library. In the early days, I was always out because I couldn't deal with being by myself. Now, six years into the divorce, I'm very comfortable being by myself. I also have a gentleman friend who I spend weekends with. Knowing he's there for me is very reassuring.

—*ANONYMOUS*
EAST BRUNSWICK, NEW JERSEY
💔25Y 💔6Y

TALK TO THE GATOR

My second husband and I were at an airport one time and I bought a little alligator. Whenever he would get upset, I would make the alligator talk to him in a funny voice: "Eh, she's being a pain. I don't understand her. What are we going to do?" And the funny thing was, he would actually talk back to the alligator. When I sent him the divorce papers, he wouldn't answer them. So I took the alligator, put it in a doll-sized pool, gagged it, and sent it to my husband with an audiotape that said, "You gotta help me, you gotta sign the papers or I don't know what's going to happen!" He signed the papers the next day.

—*FRAN*
HOWARD BEACH, NEW YORK
💔5Y 💔 💔 💔 ⚱

ONCE I REALIZED DIVORCE WAS INEVITABLE, I decided I was going to learn as much as I could about myself in the process. I knew it would still be hard, but it helped to know that there would be a positive outcome in the midst of all the uncertainty, and that all the pain wouldn't be for naught.

—KARIN TARPLEY
SEATTLE, WASHINGTON
💔4Y 💔5Y

" Cry. Cry really hard. But when you're done, be done. When one chapter is complete, be ready to move on to a new one. "

—CRISTOFFER
SAN DIEGO, CALIFORNIA

LOOK AT A DIVORCE AS A FRESH START. When I moved out, I decided that I wasn't bringing any large items with me. My husband and I had built our home together, so it had a great deal of spiritual significance for me. I felt that if I took the furniture with me, it would represent our marriage. So I decided that if I couldn't ship it, it didn't come. I left a lot of myself in that house, but I think it was the right decision for me.

—LAURA VINCENT
SAN RAFAEL, CALIFORNIA
💔20Y 💔PENDING

I JUST IMAGINED MYSELF as a Hollywood movie star. They get divorced all the time and still are so popular and glamorous. I mean, if Liz Taylor can do it, why not me? It sounds silly, but I think that helped me feel a little better about being labeled a "divorcée."

> —SHANNON L.
> SAN RAFAEL, CALIFORNIA
> 17Y 21Y

DIVORCE DATA

Current figures suggest that the time of greatest risk for divorce is the fourth year of marriage.

• • • • • • • • •

TURN OFF THE TELEVISION AND START READING. Try fiction, nonfiction, mystery, classics, comedy, and self-help, too. I gave up cable and began to read. It quieted the noise and still let me escape and dream.

> —M.H.
> SAN ANTONIO, TEXAS
> 10Y 4Y

SLEEPLESS NIGHTS

I didn't really move out so much as she threw me out. It was one of those situations where I came home from work one day, and she was in the process of gathering my things into a big suitcase. She asked me to leave immediately. I didn't want to fight in front of our son, so I left. But I had nowhere to go: I had no family in the area, and we were not well off financially. The first two nights I stayed in my car. I think my appearance at work those days raised some eyebrows. I couldn't shave, and I couldn't shower, but I was afraid if I missed work I'd be fired. My wife eventually let me back in as we worked through the problems. But I was gone for good a few months later. I'll never forget those nights in the car.

> —PERRY O'MALLEY
> HARRISONBURG, VIRGINIA
> 8Y 30Y

I WAS FINE DURING THE DAY because I was so busy, but it was so hard at night. No matter how depressed I was, I always told myself that if I could just get through the night, everything would be better in the morning.

—*BARBARA STEVENS*
GATLINBURG, TENNESSEE
💔18Y 💔 💔3Y 💔 💔28Y

· · · · · · · ·

" My wife and I had a community property divorce:
She got all of the property, and I got the heck out of the community. "

—*BOB*
SAN DIEGO, CALIFORNIA
💔21Y 💔5Y

· · · · · · · ·

PROTECT YOURSELF. Decide what is best for you, then negotiate with your ex on how to handle everything (dividing up assets, home, children, communication with each other, to go to court and fight it out or try to negotiate a separation agreement between yourselves, etc.). He is no longer your ally or partner on things, so clear your head and figure out how you want to handle these things.

—*DAWN PETCHELL*
ARLINGTON, VIRGINIA
💔2Y 💔1Y

THE HARDEST PART WAS BEING AFRAID: What am I going to do? Can I do right by the kids? I'm a very practical person. I needed to get a secure environment for myself. I got credit in my own name. I took a look at my financial situation. And I found support from my church group and neighbors.

—*KAREN*
DANA POINT, CALIFORNIA
23Y 17Y

BREAKING UP, BARBIE-STYLE

Mattel's first-quarter earnings after Barbie and Ken's "break-up" decreased 73 percent.

RENTING FIVE YEARS' WORTH of *Sex and the City* episodes was an extremely cathartic experience. That show is all about relationships and how hard they can be. It makes you realize you're not alone, which is very comforting.

—*E.C.*
NEW YORK, NEW YORK
2M 2Y

WHEN WE GOT DIVORCED, we were living in Syracuse, New York, which is his home town, and everyone knew everyone. Wherever I went, everyone knew my husband, and it was as if my private life was out there on the streets. So I got a company transfer to North Carolina. And after that I was really able to start my life over.

—*JANIS*
CARY, NORTH CAROLINA
20Y 22Y

I USED TO CRY WHEN the wind would blow. I would cry because I couldn't find a piece of paper, I would cry when I woke up to go to the bathroom in the early morning! Once you get through the tears, embarrassment, and feeling of worthlessness, you have weathered the storm.

—*STACEY SAMUELS*
CHICAGO, ILLINOIS
2Y 2Y

Grab some friends and a cocktail and know in time your life will lead you to a better place.

—*MELISSA*
MANHATTAN BEACH,
CALIFORNIA

I KEPT THINKING ABOUT the life I had before the marriage. Everything at the time was so confusing, and I was suffering from a big guilt trip. I felt hurt and awful. But then I remembered that there were people I knew who loved me. I remember one friend saying, "We just want you to be happy." So I said to myself, "Life is short and I wasn't meant to be unhappy. I'm going back to the life I had before I was married."

—*M.Z. THWAITE WEEKS*
RIVERTON, NEW JERSEY
2Y 2Y 4Y

• • • • • • • •

I REMEMBER MANY NIGHTS sitting at home watching TV and doing nothing. I wasn't dating. I wasn't interacting with people. After a while, this definitely wears on you. If I could do it over again, I would have gotten a hobby, gone back to school, or forced myself to go to the mall. Anything to be around other people. Once I finally started forcing myself out of the house, I immediately felt better.

—*DEBBIE REDDEN-BRUNELLO*
TEMECULA, CALIFORNIA
15Y 4Y

• • • • • • • •

YOU ALWAYS HEAR THAT THINGS get easier with time, but people don't tell you to expect it to be harder for the first few months. I enjoyed moving out; I was finally able to date again and to leave all of the confusion behind. But after a few months, the finality set in, and I felt a deep sense of loss. I mourned for the past I shared with my ex, but I think I cried more for the future we were building.

—*ANDREA*
NEW YORK, NEW YORK
5Y 1Y

"Can We Agree on One Thing?": Children and Divorce

If you have children, your divorce is no longer about just you and your unhappiness; it's about your kids and what will make them happiest. The toughest part might be telling them. Here's how, as well as some advice on how to handle the fallout.

WHEN MY WIFE AND I SPLIT UP, I should've told my children that our divorce had nothing to do with them. Unfortunately, I was so wrapped up in my anger toward my ex that the words got lost.

—*STEVEN GREEN*
LOS ANGELES, CALIFORNIA
💔10Y 💔19Y

REMAINING AMICABLE IS REALLY THE BEST THING FOR THE CHILDREN.

—*BECKY*
SEATTLE, WASHINGTON
💔10Y 💔3Y

HEAD LINES

Best Advice and Top Tips

- Make a plan with your spouse about how you will break the news of your divorce to the children.

- Be civil with your ex for the sake of your children, no matter how hurt and angry you are.

- Pay extra attention to your children during a divorce and reassure them that they are still loved by both parents.

- Don't use your children to get information about your ex.

- If you are the noncustodial parent, be consistent and dependable when making plans with your children.

Look at a divorce and visitation as a business transaction, so as to keep your emotions out of it while in front of the kids.

—*B.E.A.*
BLAN, OHIO
💔7Y 💔8Y

DURING A DIVORCE, children can make life seem worthwhile again. But you have to put on a happy face for them. It's not their problem that their parents are no longer together. Make sure their lives remain positive and good and that you don't create a poisonous atmosphere for them.

—*F.R.*
SYDNEY, AUSTRALIA
💔17Y 💔2Y

• • • • • • • • •

IN VERMONT THERE'S A RULE that if you have kids and want to get divorced, you have to take a Divorcing Parenting Class at the courthouse. The guidelines, as acted out by the two teachers and portrayed in a special video, demonstrated tenets like, "Don't use the kids as messengers," "Stay focused on the kids and what cool things they're into," and "Don't disrespect the other spouse (present or absent) for the kids' edification."

—*ARCH*
LONDONDERRY, VERMONT
💔18Y 💔1Y

I HAVE NEVER BEEN MORE SCARED in my life than when I had to tell the kids that their father and I were splitting up. You have to stress to them that they are loved tremendously by both parents, that they will continue to see both of you, and that the divorce had nothing to do with them whatsoever. Kids tend to blame themselves for this stuff.

—*ANGIE BULLOCK*
BARRELVILLE, MARYLAND
10Y 4Y

. . . .

' If you have children, pay attention to them during the divorce, because they are going through a harder time than you are. "

—*JOE*
LONG ISLAND, NEW YORK

. . . .

USE CHILD-CUSTODY MEDIATION. It forces parents to work together to devise a plan that is acceptable to both of them. This plan may be very structured, specifying the day-to-day time-share of the children, as well as plans for holidays, vacations, and other special issues of the family. You can avoid the battles that are so damaging to kids, and you can include the kids in the decision-making. The last thing I wanted was for my kids to think my husband and I were fighting over them. This way they had some say in how we handled it, and they both told me afterward how happy they were about that.

—*AUDRY WISNESKI*
SEWICKLEY, PENNSYLVANIA
14Y 1Y

SAFE HARBOR

If you are going through a divorce, you must have family support for your kids, because in that situation kids are like little rowboats that have been cut adrift. The parents are reeling and incapable of pulling it together, addressing huge financial concerns and all the emotional stuff.

My son went through a really hard time when his father and I were divorced. I wasn't there for him. He started having problems with school and with his nerves. But the one ray of light was that we were living in an apartment that we rented from my mother-in-law, who lived next door. My son had his grandmother to go to, and she was his surrogate mother during that time. While I was working full-time and trying to pull myself back together, my son came home from school to her house, and that was his sanctuary. Thank God for the proximity of my mother-in-law.

If someone going through divorce doesn't have family close by, I recommend moving to where they are, or figuring out some sort of arrangement to give the kids an anchor, to give them some stability.

—D.W.
SAN DIEGO, CALIFORNIA
💔11Y 💔 💔15Y

MY HUSBAND AND I DECIDED to break the news to our children together, but instead my ex took my 11-year-old son to the store and told him himself. My son definitely had the notion that Mom was leaving the family. Since then, I've had to work very hard to regain a relationship with him. Don't let any time lapse between making the decision to talk to your kids and actually doing so. I only let a couple of days go by, and I've been paying for it ever since.

> —*DEBBIE REDDEN-BRUNELLO*
> *TEMECULA, CALIFORNIA*
> 💔15Y 💔4Y

. . . .

DON'T NITPICK WITH YOUR EX over every child-rearing issue. I don't expect my ex to do everything the way I do. For example, I don't expect that the children will eat their veggies every night with Daddy, or get their hair washed every night. It'd be nice, but you have to pick your battles. If he holds their hand when they cross the street, I'm happy.

> —*DANA*
> *ANNISTON, ALABAMA*
> 💔6Y 💔 💔1Y

. . . .

KEEP AS MANY THINGS as possible the same after a divorce. I stayed in the same house. When their dad moved out with his furniture, I made sure our children were out of the house. I rearranged the furniture before they got back so it would still look like home. That was more secure and comforting to them. Also, I kept my married last name so that it would match the children's school records and there would be no confusion about who their mother was.

> —*JOBETH MCLEOD*
> *SAN ANTONIO, TEXAS*
> 💔25Y 💔5Y

ALL IN THE FAMILY

The majority of divorces occur in families with children under the age of 18.

I THINK KIDS KNOW SUBCONSCIOUSLY before you tell them—sometimes even before you've told yourself. My ex-husband and I had been seeing a family therapist with the children and decided to tell them in the therapist's office. I don't know if it was the good way or the right way. It was just the way it was.

—*A.L.*
BEVERLY HILLS, CALIFORNIA
🖤18Y 🖤 🖤1Y

· · · · · · · ·

66 Don't bad-mouth your spouse. You shouldn't tell your kids, 'I left your father because he's a bastard.' Children don't want to choose. If dad is a bastard, they will eventually find out on their own. 99

—*ANONYMOUS*
MARTINDALE, TEXAS
🖤 🖤28Y

· · · · · · · ·

 AFTER EACH VISIT, I give my ex feedback about how it went. I'll tell him if my daughter missed him afterwards, or what she said about the visit. It requires that you talk with your ex a lot, but in the end, it's so important.

—*DANA*
ANNISTON, ALABAMA
🖤6Y 🖤 🖤1Y

A TOUGH CHOICE

Our kids knew nothing of our two-year struggle. My therapist recommended not telling them. I disagree with that approach now because my daughter, who was nine years old, ended up with intestinal problems caused by the stress of feeling there was something wrong and not knowing what it was.

We sat them down after I'd made my decision and quietly told them that I was going to move out. We gave space for them to ask questions and reassured them that I would be nearby. My son, then 16, was totally unaware consciously of any problems and was shocked, but he took it quietly. My daughter was concerned but not visibly upset at first. Both were concerned about my being out on my own and about being able to have regular contact with me.

My husband and I had decided on a joint custody arrangement with him as the primary custodian. He insisted on this and I chose not to fight it because I believe that children need a home base and should not be flipping back and forth every week, like some folks do. So, they stay primarily with Dad and I get them every other weekend.

Always, always remember that you owe your children the gift of civility with your ex. Children need to heal, so the sooner you all heal your issues as much as possible, the sooner they will be able to move on and develop good long-term relationships as adults.

—J.S.
HOUSTON, TEXAS
💔20Y 💔3Y

My ex and I
agreed on all
the serious
issues, so
we're in
sync about
disciplining.
It's nice to be
able to talk
about it.

—*DANA
ANNISTON,
ALABAMA*
6Y 1Y

IF YOU TAKE CARE OF YOURSELF, your kids will be fine. My ex-husband had our sons with him on the weekends. I started playing more tennis, taught parenting classes, and spent time with my friends. I did special things for myself, like buying flowers. I also redecorated my bathroom, filling it with plants and candles. My sons called it my mystical bath.

—*SUSIE WALTON
SAN DIEGO, CALIFORNIA*
19Y 14Y

• • • • • • • •

I STOOD UP TO MY EX-HUSBAND when he had my daughter for the weekend and she got an earache. He wanted me to take her to the doctor. I said, "You will. She's your daughter and *you* will take her." I told him he doesn't just get her for the fun stuff. That approach led to their closer relationship. He even ended up as her "room mother" when I was working full-time and she was in grade school.

—*A.B.
PRAIRIE VILLAGE, KANSAS*

• • • • • • • •

IF YOU HAVE CHILDREN, don't question them about what is going on in your ex-spouse's life. This only makes your children uncomfortable, and it does nothing to foster a cordial relationship with your ex. My ex-husband had the bad habit of grilling the children on what I was up to (dating and otherwise) when they would go to visit. It got so bad that the children would become physically ill before their visits. Once we all learned how to navigate our changed relationships with one another, things got a lot better.

—*W.F.R.M.
OKLAHOMA CITY, OKLAHOMA*

MY HUSBAND AND I HAVE sort of a *Brady Bunch* family. We each have three kids from our first marriage. Both of our exes still live close by so that the kids get to spend time with their other parents. That time is really important. No matter how much we dislike our former spouses, the kids still want to spend time with them. It's good if you live close enough for that to happen.

—*DIANE SMITH*
HARMONY, PENNSYLVANIA
3Y 7Y

* * * * * * * *

MY 10-YEAR-OLD SON WROTE A POEM about having his heart ripped out called "Why Me?" He feels better now, and when he reads it I remind him that time makes everything easier.

—*ANONYMOUS*
TORONTO, ONTARIO
12Y 1Y

* * * * * * * *

SOMETIMES IT FEELS LIKE you can exact revenge on your spouse by hurting his children. But, if you are the noncustodial parent, do not withdraw or withhold child support or hide personal assets during divorce proceedings in order to hurt your spouse. It only ends up hurting the children, and they do not deserve it.

—*PEGGY WEHR*
WOODWORTH, OHIO
11Y 8Y

* * * * * * * *

YOU HAVE TO MAKE EXTRA TIME for your children, during and after your divorce. Don't even plan special events or fun things to do—spending time with them is the only thing that's important, even if it's just doing chores or going to the pool.

—*JANE*
EARLYSVILLE, VIRGINIA
15Y

DIVORCE DATA

About 1.5 million children in the United States experience the divorce of their parents each year—ultimately 40 percent of all children.

BETTER IN THE LONG RUN

It was hard not being with my son when my ex-husband and I split up. I was left with no place of my own and had to live with friends until I could afford to get my own apartment. I was working nights and going to college during the day. I didn't fight for my son because of not having a stable home for him. I cried many nights missing him; he was only five years old at the time.

After about four months, when I did get my own apartment, I filed for my divorce and decided to start my life over. I wanted to make a fresh start not just for myself, but for my son as well. My ex-husband and I fought a lot during the separation and until the end of our divorce, and we had many issues over our son. He told me to stop picking him up at school and tried to prevent me from seeing him.

Now, after almost three years since my divorce has been final, and with the perspective that has come with time, my ex-husband and I have become friends and I get to see my son whenever I like and take him anywhere I want. I remarried a little over two years ago. It has been a big adjustment for my son as well as for me, but I know we'll all be happier and healthier in the end.

> —*WANDA*
> *BALTIMORE, MARYLAND*
> 🐱11Y 💔 🐱2Y

SET A CONSISTENT SCHEDULE of visits with your children. It's better for you, and probably better for them as well. I have a 10-year-old daughter, and I find out my schedule with her week to week. I have an extra bedroom, and she's always welcome. The only problem with this arrangement is that it's difficult to find my own life. Dating is tough, because I don't always know when I'll have a "date" with my child.

—*ANONYMOUS*
SAN FRANCISCO, CALIFORNIA
7Y 5Y

. . . .

‘ It comes down to love. If one spouse wants to make things difficult, it's best to step back and think of the kids first and foremost. Conflict ultimately damages the kids. ’’

—*J.M. CORNWELL*
TABERNASH, COLORADO
13Y 22Y

. . . .

THE GREATEST THING I DID was to take a co-parenting course. The class gives parents the information, tools, and tips to remain good parents, even if they're not together anymore. Most of the time, the two parents attend together. In my case, I attended alone, but it still made a world of difference.

—*ANNE DEAN*
HUNTINGTON BEACH, CALIFORNIA
5Y 2Y

ADVICE FOR DIVORCED FATHERS

IF YOU ARE A FATHER WITH CUSTODY, you have to dive in and get as involved in your kids' lives as their mother would. You have to join the PTA and volunteer for bake sales and fund drives—even if these organizations are mostly women, you can't let that bother you. You have to do it for the kids. I even learned how to bake brownies after my divorce.

> —G.R.
> BOARDMAN, OHIO
> 10Y 2Y

• • • • • • • •

MY CHILDREN GIVE ME STRENGTH. There's no greater motivation for me to stay healthy than my kids. I belong to a group called Fathers and Families. Groups like this help dads like me vent and support each other.

> —ANONYMOUS
> WESTON, MASSACHUSETTS
> 12Y PENDING

• • • • • • • •

IT'S VERY DIFFICULT TO BE A SINGLE DAD, and I found support through nonprofit groups in the community. I would recommend scoping out these groups and making contact with them before deciding to move out, since this will alleviate some of the worry and pressure.

> —DAVE
> GREENBELT, MARYLAND
> 8Y 1Y

• • • • • • • •

WOMEN USUALLY THINK THAT their children are their possessions, but it's best to share parenting, unless the spouse is totally unworthy. You will need the time to get a job and get organized as a single person.

> —GEORGENE
> CRYSTAL BEACH, FLORIDA
> 7Y   13Y   3Y

THE DIVORCE COULD CAUSE behavioral problems with the kids. And don't be surprised if they don't surface right away. My daughter seemed fine for the first couple years, but when she turned 12 her behavior deteriorated badly. Some children might say or do hurtful things. Try to stay patient, to allow the children to talk openly and to express anger, fear, sadness, and disappointment—even if this anger or disappointment is directed at you.

—*LORRAINE KOLLAR*
WOODWORTH, OHIO
🖤13Y 🖤12Y

• • • • • • • •

NO MATTER HOW DIFFICULT your children might become, you have to stick it out. There were times that I wanted nothing to do with my son, and realizing that my failed marriage was at the root of his troubles hurt me so much. But you can't give up. Try to stay calm and in touch with your children; abandonment haunts a child forever.

—*E.H.*
SALEM, OHIO
🖤17Y 🖤3Y

• • • • • • • •

WHEN I LEFT MY WIFE, I don't think I realized that I would be taking a chance on my son not being in my life as he was before. We went through a year-long custody dispute that ended up costing more than I ever bargained for. Not only did I lose that money, I lost my son. I am now going through the rebuilding stages of my life, and, to this day, I love my son very dearly and try to see him as often as possible—although now, instead of six minutes away, it's six hours.

—*JOSEPH LEE*
SAINT PETERSBURG, FLORIDA
🖤1Y 🖤1Y

LEGACIES

In 1996, children of divorce were 50 percent more likely than their counterparts from intact families to divorce.

MY DAUGHTER HAD BEGGED ME for months to leave my husband because he was very abusive to her—more mentally than physically—and he did the same to me. I had it in my head that I would wait until she graduated and was settled in college. I did, and I've regretted not doing it sooner—much, much sooner.

—*C.*
OKLAHOMA CITY, OKLAHOMA
20Y 4Y

• • • • • • • • •

THE THING THAT BOTHERS ME MOST is when I hear a parent say something like "you're just like your mother" or "you're just like your father." That is an absolutely horrible thing to say to a child who has suffered through a divorce.

—*DENNIS RUSSO*
WOODWORTH, OHIO
14Y 14Y

• • • • • • • • •

ALWAYS KEEP YOUR COOL. Even if, as in my case, you are acting to protect your children, *keep your cool.* No matter what your wife pulls, even one bad outburst on your part—whether justified or not—will be brought up again and again!

—*KEITH*
DENVER, COLORADO
1Y   6Y 1Y

• • • • • • • • •

DON'T TELL YOUR KIDS ANYTHING BAD about their father. If you know he's a bad man, your kids will figure it out on their own. When my ex doesn't come and pick up my kids when he is supposed to, I don't say anything to my children: They will realize soon enough that he wasn't there for them.

—*T.D.*
CORALVILLE, IOWA
3Y 2Y

Putting the kids first definitely made it easier to survive my divorce. Once I decided that's what I wanted to accomplish, it wasn't hard to do.

—*B.B.*
PORTLAND, OREGON
4Y 17Y

FIVE TIPS FOR FATHERS

1. KEEP THE FOCUS ON YOUR CHILDREN. Conflicts with ex-spouses and other family members, legal problems, and other related issues can rob you and your children of precious time together. Learn to deal with the outside issues appropriately and to keep your focus on what your children need from you in the moment.

2. CONNECT WITH YOUR CHILDREN'S SCHOOL AND TEACHERS. Fathers traditionally have chosen to assume the role of outsider when it comes to school and teachers. Get involved by going to the school office, introducing yourself to your children's teachers, and having relevant mailings (report cards, etc.) sent to you.

3. BE DEPENDABLE. Because the time with your children is limited, it is critical that they be able to count on your showing up on time, and regularly, for your time together. This also applies to your presence at school functions, sporting events that your kids are involved with, etc. Being dependable goes a long way toward rebuilding a sense of emotional stability for your child.

4. PLAN, BUT BE FLEXIBLE. Planning a specific activity together is important, but your plans should not be written in stone. Be open and attentive to spontaneous ideas, especially if the ideas come from your children. Kids don't want to feel trapped into a rigid routine all the time.

5. DISCOVER SACRED ACTIVITIES. There are probably many things you can do with your children that can become very meaningful, which your children will learn to associate with your time together. Something as simple as a hike through the woods, shooting baskets together, having a hobby that you feel passionate about, etc., can become a bonding experience.

—WILLIAM DUCHON
MILFORD, CONNECTICUT
 7Y 1Y

FROM THE MOUTHS OF BABES

In case you need more guilt on your plate, we're here to help. We spoke with some children of divorce—now adults—about their experience and how it has affected them. Read at your own risk (and maybe learn something, too).

MY PARENTS DIVORCED WHEN I was about 10. That's probably the worst age possible to go through something like that. It just tore me apart. I felt like all my friends were secretly making fun of me behind my back. I think the best thing parents can do is talk to the child as much as possible, and when you think you've talked to them enough, talk some more. I had so many questions. I needed so much reassuring.

> —*TRACY*
> *BETHEL PARK, PENNSYLVANIA*
> *PARENTS DIVORCED*

. . . .

EVEN OLDER CHILDREN NO LONGER LIVING AT HOME are traumatized by the divorce of their parents. I found it to be the most traumatic event of my life, more traumatic than losing my only sibling, my sister, and her husband in an auto accident, more than losing one of my best friends to AIDS, and more than the deaths of both of my parents.

> —*SARALYN*
> *CHICAGO, ILLINOIS*
> 💑28Y 💔10Y

. . . .

MY PARENTS GOT A DIVORCE WHEN I was young. It's important for kids to have someone professional to help them get through it. Children should talk about their feelings a lot. I talked with my mom, and now we have a great relationship. I didn't talk with my dad, and now we don't.

> —*T.F.*
> *MINNEAPOLIS, MINNESOTA*
> *PARENTS DIVORCED*

MY PARENTS GOT DIVORCED and both tried to win me over: to make me think that they were perfect and the other parent was wrong. That is a terrible thing to do to your kid.

> —*K.*
> *BELLEVUE, WASHINGTON*
> *PARENTS DIVORCED*

MY PARENTS GOT DIVORCED WHEN I was 14. It still hurts, but it got a little easier to deal with as I got older. I wish they had talked to me about their problems right off the bat. Who had more to lose in the situation than I did? Don't keep your kids in the dark: They have a right to know what's going on.

> —*BOB SCHULTZ*
> *HOPEWELL, PENNSYLVANIA*
> *PARENTS DIVORCED*

ONE POSITIVE THING IS that you get twice the amount of presents! The bad news is that you might have to have two Thanksgiving, Easter, and Christmas celebrations. And if your parents live in separate towns, it can become very exhausting. But it is worth it to see them both.

> —*KRISTEN*
> *SEATTLE, WASHINGTON*
> *PARENTS DIVORCED*

THE BEST THING TO COME OUT of my parents' divorce is the wonderful family that I gained when my dad remarried. You can never have too much family in life.

> —*J.D.*
> *LOS ANGELES, CALIFORNIA*
> *PARENTS DIVORCED*

WHEN I WAS 10, my father took me to a park to explain that things weren't working between him and my mom. I had already sensed this was the case for a few years, because there was always so much tension and fighting at our house. But hearing him openly admit this made me feel appreciated and respected, like we were on the same page. This doesn't mean you need to share the fine points with your kids. Just don't beat around the bush. Trust me, no matter how young the children are, they already know.

—ROBYN MURAMOTO
CENTENNIAL, COLORADO
PARENTS DIVORCED 35 YEARS

IF SPLITTING CUSTODY, work with your spouse on what you want to teach the child. If one parent wants to teach a child that R-rated movies are restricted for a reason, having the other parent allow it can wreak havoc on the kid. Allowing things like this might garner you a little favoritism, but all it does is teach the child to play their parents against each other to get what they want.

—GEOFF SHREVE
SAN DIEGO, CALIFORNIA
PARENTS DIVORCED

KEEP ON GOOD TERMS with your ex-spouse for the benefit of your children. Don't try to exclude him or her from school activities. When there were dance shows or rehearsal meals, I would invite my ex so he could be a part of my daughter's life. We had joint custody, but he didn't exercise all the visitation that he could have. I put myself and my feelings aside to make sure he and the children had a relationship.

—*ANONYMOUS*
SAN ANTONIO, TEXAS
🖤25Y ❤️5Y

• • • • • • • •

SPLIT-UP STAT

Sixty percent of children of divorce have trouble with social relationships.

NO DATING, NO NEXT MARRIAGE: Devote your full time to your children. Children need to be loved, and they need to know their father as well as their mother. They need to be talked to, guided, and disciplined by both. This works because they never lose the love for either parent, they never lose the respect for either parent, and they know that both parents are there for them.

—*DOMINGO IVAN CASANAS*
ANTIOCH, CALIFORNIA
🖤14Y ❤️ 🖤2Y

• • • • • • • •

AFTER OUR DIVORCE, my ex-wife moved to Texas with my son, and suddenly I was left with this huge void every day when I came home from work. To remedy this, I call my son two times a day and visit him three or four times each month. Every time we talk on the phone, I make sure to tell him that I love him. Doing this helps assure him that, even though his momma and I are no longer together, he still plays an extremely important role in my life.

—*ROBERT HARRIS*
LOS ANGELES, CALIFORNIA
🖤15Y ❤️5Y

Dads, if there
is a parent-
teacher
conference,
guess what?
You are still
a parent.

—KYLE
  FAIRFIELD,
  CONNECTICUT
  ♥13Y ♥7Y

MY DAUGHTER WAS COLLEGE-AGED, confident, and mature when her dad and I started going through the divorce. I saw her crumble and become a little girl again. When it was time to tell her everything, I had to spoon-feed her at first, but I knew I had to tell her the truth so she could understand it.

> —ANONYMOUS
>   KNOXVILLE, TENNESSEE
>   ♥25Y ♥ ♥1Y

• • • • • • • •

REMEMBER THAT WHATEVER YOU SAY about your marriage or your ex will most likely, even 30 years from now, get back to your ex or your children. And take it from me: Hearing something negative about your parents 30 years after their divorce can still be very painful.

> —ALEXIS
>   KNOXVILLE, TENNESSEE
>   ♥5Y ♥2Y

• • • • • • • •

WHEN YOU AREN'T THE CUSTODIAL PARENT, you have to make sure you connect with your kids. That means doing fun things that the everyday parent can't always justify doing. You do the things they want to do, like playing miniature golf, going to amusement parks, or making ice cream. It gives you a chance to bond.

> —KIM L. JAFFE
>   REDMOND, WASHINGTON
>   ♥8Y ♥ ♥27Y

• • • • • • • •

IT WAS UNUSUAL FOR A DAD to have custody when I got divorced, but there was never any question that my daughter was going to live with me. The lifestyle that her mother wanted didn't involve a child.

> —ANONYMOUS
>   SIKESTON, MISSOURI
>   ♥15Y ♥ ♥6Y

KUDOS TO GOOD PARENTS

After my parents divorced, my mother took the everyday responsibilities—the tough stuff—while my dad lived his life and visited with us about once every month or two. I played baseball, and my mother was the Team Mom each year, which meant she took care of all the kids on the team, kept score of games, wrote the newsletter each week. But during each season, my dad would show up for a game with his camera and he would take these great pictures of me playing. He was really into photography: His camera was top-quality, with a great zoom. My baseball friends always gathered around and asked him to take pictures of them. Then, after his visit, he would send me the pictures. It was something we bonded over; he would point out the ones he liked the best. But I think the interesting thing is that my mother allowed this to happen without making any snide comments about how he was walking into our baseball world and stealing the scene. She would do nothing except frame the pictures or put them in a photo album. I guess the moral is, you can be the everyday parent or the occasional parent and still do something that means a lot to your kids. What's most important is that the parents simply get along when they're around each other.

—J.W.A., III
ATLANTA, GEORGIA
PARENTS DIVORCED 34 YEARS

MY EX-HUSBAND AND I DIVORCED when our son was two years old. My son noticed his dad's absence and would become very quiet and sit by the window waiting for his dad to come up the block. I took my son to a child psychologist, and she suggested that I work with him on labeling his emotions so that he would be able to identify his fear of abandonment later in life. Now, at seven years old, my son can say he's mad or angry and can express and sort out his feelings.

—*D.L.*
CHICAGO, ILLINOIS
❤6Y ❤5Y

• • • • • • • •

" Don't make the children into footballs. It's about putting yourself third, fourth, fifth, sixth, and last, and the children first. You can't become obsessed with winning. "

—*MEL MILLER*
BRISBANE, AUSTRALIA
❤6Y ❤ ❤13Y

• • • • • • • •

AFTER THE DIVORCE, not only should you allow teenagers to keep their relationships with grandparents, aunts, uncles, etc., but you should promote them. Send a clear message that even though their family structure has changed, family is still important.

—*TIM LAKE*
BADEN, PENNSYLVANIA
❤27Y ❤3Y

BECAUSE I HAD BEEN THE PARENT who stayed home with the kids, we split custody fifty-fifty. That was by mutual agreement. That was the hardest thing for me in the process—to suddenly be with them half as much as I had been used to. As the kids have gotten older, we've told them they can spend more time with one of us or the other, but so far, they've preferred to keep the fifty-fifty arrangement.

—*J.S.*
WYNDMOOR, PENNSYLVANIA
❤20Y ❤1Y

• • • • • • • •

FATHER'S DAY IN COURT

Men win custody in 60 to 70 percent of all child custody cases that go to court.

AROUND THE AGE OF FIVE, my son went through this period where he wanted his father and me to get back together. He'd tell his dad, "Take Mom to a jewelry shop and then she'll love you again." So we spent a lot of time explaining to him that we both loved him and that he's in our hearts, and that we also love each other, but not in a married way. We emphasized that we were still a family, and we all care about each other. He has processed it very well. In his kindergarten class, when he was the star of the week, one of the girls asked during his presentation if his parents were divorced. He said yes, and explained it just like we did to him: that we were all still a family, even if Mom and Dad didn't live together anymore.

—*SALLY*
KIRKLAND, WASHINGTON

• • • • • • • •

AS A PARENT, your child is not there to be your therapist. They aren't there to listen to you whine and complain about the other parent. This will only cause them to feel pressure to pick a favorite, and it puts them in a horrible position. Remember that you have friends to vent to.

—*JENNY*
SAN FRANCISCO, CALIFORNIA

DO'S AND DON'TS WITH KIDS, FROM A VETERAN

Understand that your older children will be very uncertain about their future. Against this backdrop, consider these points:

1. You still need to be a parent and address issues with your children. Let them know that you don't have all the answers and it is OK to say, "I don't know."

2. Don't make them choose sides. If you are having a bad moment, don't criticize your spouse to your children. Make it very comfortable for your children to remain neutral.

3. Your children are not your spies. Asking questions like, "Does your father have a girlfriend yet?" and "Did your mother have a drink while you were there?" puts your children in the middle.

4. Your children are *not* a weapon. Asking questions like, "Do you love me or Daddy more?" or "If you loved your Daddy, you would want to spend this weekend with him" are the highest acts of cruelty, in my opinion.

5. Your children are not to be spoiled. Many divorcing parents overcompensate with material things to make up for the whole situation. Indulging your children's every whim is not the answer.

6. If your children throw a tantrum, let them. They might need to vent as much as you do. After the emotions of the moment have passed, they will be able to look at the situation realistically.

    —*PAUL EVERITT*
    LOUISVILLE, COLORADO
    PARENTS DIVORCED 30 YEARS

I HAVE TWO BOYS, and in some respects I think the divorce actually made them stronger people. They had to deal with adversity early and had to learn to land on their feet. And, in a sense, that's not a bad thing. So, while I wouldn't say divorce is fine, I also wouldn't say that it's always a huge negative for kids. It's better than the parents staying together when they really are not suited for each other.

> —ANONYMOUS
> BOULDER, COLORADO
> 💔4Y 💔7Y

. . . .

WHEN YOU'RE SENDING YOUR KIDS to visit your ex, don't send them empty-handed, expecting that your ex will have the things they need. When you send the children on their visits, give them what they need. If your ex does not send the clothing or items back, explain that you send the children with what they need so the visits will be pleasant for everyone, and that the children need these things returned so they will feel good about both parents.

> —DOM GRECO
> POLAND, OHIO
> 💔5Y 💔17Y

. . . .

DROPPING OFF AND PICKING UP your children can be really emotional, especially at the beginning of a separation. One way to make it less emotional is to pick up or drop off the kids at school, where you won't encounter your ex. Keep the dropping off and picking up of your kids upbeat. It is OK to tell them how happy you are to see them, or that you missed them. It is never OK to cry; suck it up. We are the reason our children are in this situation.

> —ALEXIS
> KNOXVILLE, TENNESSEE
> 💔5Y 💔2Y

Don't bad-mouth your ex to your children. Don't shoot arrows at each other because, I promise you, they go straight through your kids' hearts.

> —S.P.
> NEW YORK,
> NEW YORK
> 💔22Y 💔10Y

SIDE EFFECTS

Children between the ages of three and five years old are most likely to blame themselves for a divorce.

AS MUCH AS I WANTED TO FIGHT for full custody, I knew that this would cause the children too much pain because they love their father. In all honesty, he wasn't a bad man, and he was actually a pretty good father to them. It would be easy to let pettiness and the desire to hurt your ex-spouse cloud your judgment, but my advice is to avoid that urge.

—*JENNY*
SAN FRANCISCO, CALIFORNIA

. . . .

AFTER MY 11-YEAR-OLD DAUGHTER found out that we were getting divorced, she was angry. She didn't talk a lot. She tried to stay in her room. Her grades started slipping. She withdrew from everyone. I tried talking to her, and she said nothing was wrong. I tried spending time with her and rewarding good behavior and good grades more than before. She started becoming the person she used to be. I realized that if your kids see you upset, they will be upset, too. If they see you happy, they will be happy, too.

—*JENNIFER WEST*
GREENVILLE, MISSOURI
💔 *12Y* 💔 *1Y*

. . . .

DON'T GET RID OF all of your wedding and family photos, especially if you have kids. Put them away if you need to, but hang on to them. Kids don't have the skills and experience to handle loss and unknowns in life. You have to reassure them that things are going to be OK. It's important for kids to see photos of their parents when they were together so that the kids understand that they were conceived in love and were not a mistake.

—*IRENE VARLEY*
SARASOTA, FLORIDA
💔 *22Y* 💔 *17Y*

WHEN TO TELL THE KIDS

We had decided to tell the kids during the summer, but we had planned a family vacation. I waited until we got back, right before school started. We sat them down and told them that we had been having a lot of fights and arguments and didn't want to live our lives like that. We thought it would be best if we divorced. My daughter cried and tried to bargain with us to just get separated. She was just starting middle school, a new environment with new people. She was embarrassed and didn't want anyone to know. I told her that she might not want to tell some people, but true friends are the ones you tell things to so they can help you through the hard times.

As awful as the whole situation was, I think we did it well. We were honest with our kids. And I'm glad I took the time to sit with the information myself before I told the kids. It made me more sure in my heart that we were doing the right thing for every member of the family.

—ANONYMOUS
SEATTLE, WASHINGTON
18Y PENDING

WRITE IT DOWN

My daughter was six months old at the time of the divorce. One of the best things I did for myself was keep a journal. I wrote to my daughter. I told her things that were going on—the good and the bad. There were days when my ex stopped over, and they had a decent visit. I shared my feelings about him. I wrote about funny little things my daughter did that day. It was a record of things going on. There were some entries where I was really mad. Sometimes, I'd be bawling while I was writing. I spent a lot of time crying. To write those things down was more of a release than crying myself to sleep. I was seeing a counselor at the time. I told her I was doing this. She thought it was the greatest idea. She was going to advise others to do that. So, write things down for yourself and your children. It was a release for me, and if my daughter does want to know everything that happened someday, I'll be able to look at my journal or let her read it.

—DEBBIE L.
CAMILLUS, NEW YORK
12Y

TALK TO YOUR EX ABOUT ESTABLISHING a bedtime for the kids that you will both uphold. That way neither one is looked upon as the good parent for letting them stay up late, and neither is the bad parent, either.

—*J.H.*
POLAND, OHIO
👶5 💔 👶1Y

• • • • • • • •

If you want to go to big events in your children's lives—like graduations and weddings—make sure you don't hate your ex-spouse. It can ruin those events for you. ,,

—*J.C.*
WICHITA, KANSAS
👶 💔 👶 💔

• • • • • • • •

AS TEMPTING AS IT MIGHT BE, don't put the other parent down. In fact, it's important to honor the other parent. I admit, this was challenging for me at times. My sons visited my ex-husband on the weekends, and he didn't want them to watch TV at his home. So, they called me to vent. I knew that I had a choice. I could tell them, "Yes, he's an idiot. That's why I divorced him." Or I could support him and say, "That's the rule. Find other things to do." I chose the high ground, and it was the right thing to do.

—*S.*
SAN DIEGO, CALIFORNIA
👶19Y 💔14Y

TO GIVE MY DAUGHTER A SENSE of stability in my divorce, I show her over and over again that her mother and I will work together to do everything we can for her. To that end, I always behave in a friendly manner to my ex in front of her, and never say a harsh word about my ex or my ex's family around her.

> —*DAVID LODGE*
> *OKLAHOMA CITY, OKLAHOMA*
> 🌼6Y 💔1Y

ALLOW THE CHILDREN TO TAKE THEIR TOYS, clothing, and stuff with them if they want as they go back and forth between their parents' homes. Do not tell the children something must stay at your home because you paid for it.

> —*SUE LASKY*
> *POLAND, OHIO*
> 🌼2Y 💔11Y

DON'T PUMP YOUR KIDS FOR INFORMATION after they get back from a visit with their other parent. Have some self-respect. It makes you look pathetic to the kids, and you won't feel good about it either. It will only delay your moving on with your life.

> —*CHARLOTTE KUBALY*
> *POLAND, OHIO*
> 🌼13Y 💔3Y

WHAT I LEARNED EARLY ON after the divorce is how much my visits meant to my kids. I had to cancel a couple, and they were devastated. You have to make these visits the focus of your life. Avoid canceling planned visitations. Remember that these visits are crucial to your child's self-esteem.

> —*DAVID TRENT*
> *WOODWORTH, OHIO*
> 🌼15Y 💔6Y

"We Have Some News": Friends, Family, and Your Divorce

Then there are The Others—family and friends. And like the movie of the same name, figuring out how to deal with them can certainly haunt you. First, you have to find a good way to break the news that you're breaking up. Then, you have to listen to them tell you what a mistake they thought it was all along. And then there's your ex's family, who treats you like another horror film: The Exorcist. Before you get sick, here's how to deal with this scary business, and even come out of it on the winning side.

WHEN ONE PERSON FINDS OUT, it spreads like wildfire. You don't have to tell anyone. They already know before the day is out.

—JENNIFER WEST
GREENVILLE, MISSOURI
💔12Y 💔1Y

THE BIG PROBLEM IS WHEN OTHERS GET INVOLVED. DON'T LET OTHERS INTERFERE.

—PEDRO
AUSTIN, TEXAS
💔10Y 💔28Y

I lost all my friends who were couples, and my family thought I was crazy. Only time and distancing helped the healing.

—*GEORGENE*
  CRYSTAL BEACH,
  FLORIDA
  🌼*7Y* 💔 🌼*13Y*
  💔 🌼*3Y*

BEFORE I TOLD MY MOTHER about the divorce, I was thinking that I had the same feeling when I was about to tell her that I was pregnant: that same sense of nervous anticipation. The only way to do it is just to come out and say it. And don't be surprised if the people closest to you say that they had an inkling that something was wrong. It's hard to keep that stuff from the people who really love you.

—*A.P.*
  CORRIGANVILLE, MARYLAND
  🌼*3Y* 💔*10Y*

• • • • • • • •

I TOLD EACH PERSON IN MY LIFE as I felt ready; not everyone took it well. Many people were not surprised, especially those who really knew what my marriage was like. The people who loved me for who I was were sad, but they were also very accepting of my choice. The hardest ones to deal with were the people who judged my choice and told me what they thought even before I asked. I lost a lot of friends, but I found out who my real friends were. Also, that made room for new friends!

—*LESLIE YOUNG*
  TACOMA, WASHINGTON
  🌼*7Y* 💔*1Y*

• • • • • • • •

WHEN I TOLD MY FAMILY, I knew they would not be happy, and I knew the dangers of their taking sides or getting in the middle of things. I had a plan for what I would and would not tell them before I went into the situation. Don't enter into a discussion about it. You are not discussing it; you are simply informing them of your decision. End of story.

—*ALEXIS*
  KNOXVILLE, TENNESSEE
  🌼*5Y* 💔*2Y*

TELLING YOUR FRIENDS is completely different from telling your family. With family, you often feel some shame and guilt, as if you did something wrong. But friends often feel happy for you because they've seen the pain you have been going through. People tend to keep that from their families and save it for their friends.

　　—MARK WALBURN
　　MIDLAND, MARYLAND
　　2Y 1Y

. . . .

'It was very tough for me to tell people. I called people up a few at a time, but I mainly hoped they'd find out by word of mouth. ''

　　—PENNY PHIPPS
　　TUCSON, ARIZONA
　　12Y 15Y

. . . .

NOT MANY PEOPLE CAN TAKE the brunt of dealing with their friends going through a divorce. Why give the entire job to them? They have enough to deal with on their own. I shared a bit of pain with each of my friends. Involving different people helped me to dissipate the frustration quicker through different perspectives. Also, seeking out a professional counselor took the responsibility of "keeper of the ill will" off my friends and placed it on somebody who was getting paid to help me deal with it.

　　—CHRIS
　　SAN DIEGO, CALIFORNIA

HEADLINES
Best Advice and Top Tips

- Remember that divorcing your spouse also means divorcing your in-laws.

- Prepare yourself for the fact that many of your friends will take sides—and it won't always be the side you expect.

- Rather than telling everyone yourself, it might be easier to ask one trusted friend to spread the news of your divorce.

- Get advice on breaking the news from friends who have been through their own divorce.

- Don't allow reactions from friends and family to make you second-guess your decision to divorce.

I DON'T KNOW THAT I'D ADVISE THIS for everyone, but I had a friend who threw a party and then told us all when we got there. It was really kind of bizarre. You could see how sad he really was underneath. It was like he was whistling through the graveyard. But he had some terrific food there.

—*ANONYMOUS*
CORRIGANVILLE, MARYLAND
💔2Y 💔2Y

• • • • • • • •

ONCE I LEFT HIM, his family didn't want anything to do with me. I tried to talk to them and explain why I was filing for divorce. I even went over to his parents' house, but they wouldn't see me. I was sick about it. Eventually, I just had to accept that they were never going to understand where I was coming from. I forgave myself and moved on.

—*ANGIE*
OZARK, MISSOURI
💔1Y 💔 💔5Y

TAKING TIME TO CARE

When I told family and friends about my divorce, I went down the list, just like when someone dies. I called my parents; they were completely floored. After that, I called my youngest daughter's godfather. He drove over within 20 minutes of getting the news, with an overnight bag. He called his wife, who was on a business trip in Europe, to find out what to say to me. His wife said, "Just listen and hold her tight and make sure she calls me, too, even if it is 4 a.m. in Europe." The next day, after church, I called my husband's college roommate and his wife. On Monday, I got to work and wrote e-mails to all my children's godparents and simply stated that my husband "wants a divorce. He has found love and comfort with another woman. Please pray for me and the girls. We need your moral support. Call or write me back when you can digest all this news." I needed time to absorb everything that had happened, and I knew that all my friends did as well. Within the next two days, I had talked to all of them personally for about an hour each. They took the time to listen. They took the time to care. They all asked, "What can I do for you today?"

—KATRINA PIPASTS
PARK RIDGE, ILLINOIS
💔17Y 💔3Y

I MADE A POINT TO CALL on one person I knew who had been through a divorce herself, who could understand what I was going through. It's especially important to tell people about your divorce who are healthy themselves. Don't reach out to people who are filled with negativity. A healthy person will commiserate with you, but they will also help you to see that life will get better, that it won't always be this way.

—*IRENE VARLEY*
SARASOTA, FLORIDA
💔22Y 💔17Y

• • • • • • • •

WHEN MY WIFE AND I GOT DIVORCED, we asked each other how we would tell our parents. We agreed that we would tell them together. We had never heard of anyone doing that before; it was our idea. They didn't take it well, but at least they heard it from both of us. In this way, they looked at both of us as the cause of our breakup, instead of my parents looking at her as the cause and her mother looking at me as the cause.

—Z.
HELLERTOWN, PENNSYLVANIA
💔4Y 💔

SOME SECOND THOUGHTS

According to a *Divorce* magazine online poll, 80 percent of divorced women say if they could change the past, they still would have gotten divorced, but only 58 percent of divorced men say they would have done so.

I PUT TOGETHER AN ANNOUNCEMENT and mailed it out to my friends and family, telling them that it was with sadness that I must announce that my husband and I were getting a divorce, that we knew it was the best course for us, and that we thank them for their wishes. I was surprised by the number of people who called me right away, offering their support. I was grateful that I had been able to tell them what was happening in my own words, rather them hearing it whisper-down-the-alley style.

—*SHARON NAYLOR*
MADISON, NEW JERSEY
6Y 6Y

. . . .

I DIDN'T WANT TO HEAR all the "I told you so's." But what I found was that people were much more concerned about my emotional well-being than anything else. Everyone was very support-ive. If I had known that in advance, I wouldn't have spent so much time worrying about what everyone else would think of me.

—*DANIEL H. AMINOFF*
ALEXANDRIA, VIRGINIA
6Y 4Y

. . . .

CHOOSE YOUR TIMING CAREFULLY when telling people about your divorce. If you're the initiator and you tell people too soon—before you've made up your mind completely—you run the risk of them kicking you to a place you weren't ready to go. Along the same lines, when you tell people whom you're very close to about your divorce, be gentle with them; the divorce is likely to affect them and cause them pain, too. No matter what, telling people about your divorce is going to make it all the more real for you.

—*ANONYMOUS*
AMHERST, MASSACHUSETTS

> The few friends I had were so supportive that I felt even better about myself. They helped when I needed help, and did things that people don't do for just anybody.
>
> —*M.K.*
> *MARIETTA, GEORGIA*
> PENDING

WHEN YOUR FRIENDS ARE WENCHES . . .

Over the years, in the art community of downtown Los Angeles, my beautiful loft and garden had been the center of all life rituals and gatherings for me and the women who lived nearby. We called them Wench Fests. We came together to celebrate births, weddings, transitions of all sorts—even death.

When my departure, thanks to my divorce, became real to my dear wenches, an unusual gathering was planned by them, a first for all of us: a break-up ritual! My friends were in mourning for my leaving and yet they felt that a celebration of my bravery and positive step away from a bad situation was the most vital thing they could offer me.

When I entered the loft, the first thing I saw was a circle of candles and rose petals with a decorated chair in the center. On the chair was a handmade crown. Next, I saw a dress form in the center of an altar of flowers with a T-shirt that read, "Dump Him!" I burst out laughing.

When I took my center seat, they read a proclamation that honored me for doing the difficult work required for such a journey. I was moving to the East Coast, and they gave me warm clothes, gas money, and many necessary items for my cross-country trip: a case of red wine, a French press with excellent coffee for the series of hotel rooms I was about to face, flashlights, and an atlas (with the most direct route to my destination already marked!), books on tape, and talismans for my dashboard altar.

It was a glorious, one-of-a-kind event. As much as we cried, we were all filled with strength in the presence of so much love and support.

—HAWLEY HUSSEY
BROOKLYN, NEW YORK
🐢 ❤2Y

I WAS SURPRISED HOW HARD IT WAS with some of my girlfriends. They actually felt betrayed that I didn't tell them sooner. I think it's a girl thing, and to a degree I understand it. Girlfriends tell each other everything. If one of them doesn't know something first—whether it's about an engagement, a pregnancy, or a divorce—she can end up with hurt feelings.

> —A.L.
> BEVERLY HILLS, CALIFORNIA
> 18Y 1Y

· · · · · · · ·

" In an age of e-mail, it might be easier to just make a blanket announcement. Back in the '70s, we didn't make it a point to call everyone in our phone book: We just told people as we encountered them. "

> —HAROLD JAFFE
> REDMOND, WASHINGTON
> 16Y 26Y

· · · · · · · ·

IT WAS RATHER UNCOMFORTABLE to tell people that we were getting divorced. A lot of the people I knew did not like my wife, but I wanted sympathy; it was something that had saddened and hurt me. But all my friends were like, "Yeah! Awesome! Finally!" That was not the reaction I wanted.

> —BEN BROWN
> AUSTIN, TEXAS

MAKE SURE YOU TALK TO any mutual friends you have as early as possible. You want to get your side of the story in before your spouse tells them lies. There were a couple of people who wouldn't speak to me after the divorce because they believed what she told them about me. It wasn't true, but she got to them first.

—*WALKER EDWARDS*
CANFIELD, OHIO
5Y 8Y

• • • • • • • • •

I DIDN'T WANT ANYONE TO KNOW that I was getting a divorce. I didn't bring it up. If someone asked, I would tell them that things just didn't work out, then I would change the subject. I didn't go into a lot of detail. People don't need to know everything about your personal life.

—*ANGIE*
OZARK, MISSOURI
1Y   5Y

• • • • • • • • •

LEAN HARD ON ANYBODY OR ANYTHING that can take the strain. That does not mean you should lean on your kids: It does mean your family, your church, synagogue, mosque or temple, your friends, your boss, any support groups in the area, and the Internet.

—*RYAN YOUNG*
EL CERRITO, CALIFORNIA
5Y 4Y

• • • • • • • • •

ONCE I GOT SMART and dumped my husband, I realized I didn't have to play nice with his relatives anymore. I put up with their crap for years just to keep the peace. After the divorce, the gloves came off.

—*JANET DOMBROUS*
POLAND, OHIO
8Y 7Y

Have a friend in another time zone. Mine was in Australia, so in the middle of the night there was always someone I could call.

—*HANIA*
SEATTLE,
WASHINGTON
1Y 3Y

JUST WHAT YOU WANTED TO HEAR?

PLEASE DON'T TELL ME IT WASN'T MY FAULT. That's the number one thing people want to say. I'm supposed to believe that I'm perfect and he's a total jerk? Let's be realistic: We were both at fault. You're not helping me at all by saying that. Just tell me I'll eventually get over it.

> —ERICA GRAHAM
> ACCIDENT, MARYLAND
> ♥7Y ♥2Y

• • • • • • • • •

"YOUR EX IS AN IDIOT." That just makes me feel like a moron for marrying her in the first place. I'd rather have someone say, "You guys are both cool, but you just weren't right for each other."

> —JONATHAN BARNES
> CUMBERLAND, MARYLAND
> ♥4Y ♥3Y

• • • • • • • • •

DON'T SAY, "THESE THINGS TAKE TIME." When I was first going through my divorce, every day seemed to last about three and a half days. Time seemed to mean nothing to me. I couldn't keep track of the days of the week. It was like going through the grieving process.

> —WILLIAM GREEN
> FROSTBURG, MARYLAND
> ♥4Y ♥2Y

I HAD A FRIEND who was incredibly willing to go out on a Tuesday night and just talk and have beers. I never really told him the whole story of my divorce, but he knew I was going through something. He never wanted details, which was good. But I met all my new friends because he was willing to help introduce me to people.

—*EVAN*
ATLANTA, GEORGIA
1Y 5Y

. . . .

IF YOU CAN MAINTAIN A RELATIONSHIP with your in-laws, it's wonderful. Not having as much contact with my in-laws after my divorce was one of my greatest losses. But through phone and e-mail, I have maintained a wonderful relationship with them. My second husband and I went to their 50th wedding anniversary celebration recently, and they're coming to my son's upcoming wedding. My second husband and I have a daughter together, and my former in-laws accept her as their grandchild as well.

—*PENNY PHIPPS*
TUCSON, ARIZONA
12Y 15Y

. . . .

WHEN MY HUSBAND AND I DECIDED to separate and my friends and family thought there was a chance of reconciliation, they didn't say much to me; they didn't want to be in an awkward position of saying something negative should we get back together. However, when I told them that we were definitely divorcing, they were relieved that I chose not to stay with him. It turns out that the problems we had in our marriage were evident to them from the beginning and I just didn't see them.

—*DAWN PETCHELL*
ARLINGTON, VIRGINIA
2Y 1Y

BE PREPARED FOR YOUR IN-LAWS to side with your spouse. My relationship with my in-laws was one of the hardest things for me to let go of after my divorce. I didn't have a close family, and I considered my in-laws to be my family.

—IRENE VARLEY
SARASOTA, FLORIDA
22Y 17Y

* * * * * * * *

PEOPLE WILL EVENTUALLY SHOW their allegiance to the party that they were originally friends with. There are friends that you brought to the marriage, and friends that she brought to the marriage. Those people are obviously going to stay with their original friends after the marriage. And friends that you made together, after you were married, were still brought to the relationship by one partner or the other.

—REGGIE BONFIELD
FROSTBURG, MARYLAND
6Y 9Y

* * * * * * * *

SPREAD OUT YOUR GRIEF among your friends. If you constantly talk with only one friend about your pain, by the time you're divorced she won't want to see you ever again.

—ANONYMOUS
AMHERST, MASSACHUSETTS

* * * * * * * *

IT MIGHT NOT BE AS HARD as you think to tell your friends and family about your divorce. In the long run, your closest friends and family come through and only want what's best for you.

—G.D.V.
PRINCETON, NEW JERSEY
22Y PENDING

THOSE WHO WANT TO STAY FRIENDS with you, will. Those you don't want to stay friends with you, won't. It was a way for me to find out which of my friends really cared about me. Some people just drifted away, and that's fine; you don't want people hanging around if they really don't care about you.

—*J.L.*
WOODLAND, MARYLAND
💔*2Y* 💔*8Y*

• • • • • • • •

WHEN MY WIFE AND I SPLIT UP, I divorced our mutual friends as well. Keeping in touch was out of the question; the pain associated with that community was just too great. In order to make a clean break, I needed to start fresh by moving to a new location and making new friends.

—*BOB*
SAN DIEGO, CALIFORNIA
💔*21Y* 💔*5Y*

THE SECRET DIVORCE

I think it's important that you and your spouse each let your own families and friends know about your divorce. But it is not always the case, and there are no guarantees that your spouse will be as open as you are with communications. I let my family and friends know about my separation and intentions to divorce soon after it occurred, and I expected my husband to do the same. To my surprise, six months later, my in-laws still didn't know!

Unfortunately, my mother-in-law only found out after an address card for a magazine gift subscription she gave me was returned to her with my new address. I guess this should not have been a surprise to me; my husband was never very forthcoming with his family.

—*G.D.V.*
PRINCETON, NEW JERSEY
💔*22Y* 💔*PENDING*

I HAVE NOT COMMUNICATED WITH my former in-laws at all. It makes it easier.

> —*ANONYMOUS*
> *KENT, WASHINGTON*
> 💔8Y 💔5Y

· · · · · · · · ·

" When you get divorced, you have to change your friends and change your life. Sometimes people you thought were your friends were really your spouse's, and now they're no longer friends with you. "

> —*ANONYMOUS*
> *CHICAGO, ILLINOIS*
> 💔10Y 💔 💔8Y 💔5Y

· · · · · · · · ·

I'D BEEN GOOD FRIENDS WITH my in-laws, but during the divorce we stopped communicating. My ex-husband and my in-laws all thought I was horrible because it didn't look to them like I was sad about the marriage breaking up. About two years after the divorce, I wrote them a letter and told them I really cared about them, and I apologized for anything I had done to hurt them. I told them how difficult the divorce had been for me, even though I'd put on a façade and it looked to everyone like I was busy and having a great time. My in-laws wrote back and told me they cared about me, too, and the relationship was healed.

> —*LAURIE C.*
> *SAN DIEGO, CALIFORNIA*

I HAVE LOST ALL MY FRIENDS AND FAMILY, except for my father, with this divorce, leaving me with no support system. This was because I was never my own person during the relationship; our friends were really just his friends. Some of these people used to even call me and harass me.

—*MONICA WILLETT*
FORT MYERS, FLORIDA
💔*12Y* 💔*1M*

• • • • • • • •

" Watch out for the people who tell you right away that they plan on staying friends with both of you: That's a sure sign that they will side with your spouse. "

—*BILL DAUGHERTY*
FROSTBURG, MARYLAND
💔 💔*13Y*

• • • • • • • •

MY FRIEND AND I WERE BOTH going through a divorce and we helped keep each other busy. She wanted to paint some rooms in her house, and she had spackled holes the size of Cincinnati. We were sanding for three hours; it got so bad she had to have somebody else finish the rooms. It was good to know that if I was desperate to do something, she was there for me. There was no time to sit in the bed and cry. We had stuff to do.

—*MARYANN GABRIEL*
FRANKLIN, MASSACHUSETTS
💔*2Y* 💔 💔*15Y*

HERE'S WHERE THE PROBLEM COMES IN: You met someone and hit it off, and then you went out as couples, and your husband and her husband also became fast friends. Now the men are friends, but they only know each other because of the original relationship between the women. That puts the men in a tough spot after the divorce. As the ex-wife, you have to be the bigger person and not cause problems if they want to remain friends. Don't ask your girlfriend why her husband keeps hanging out with your deadbeat ex. Always take the high road and it will lead you to better places.

—*TAMMY NELSON*
MIDLOTHIAN, MARYLAND
💔5Y 💔9Y

. . . .

IF YOU ARE CLOSE TO MEMBERS OF your ex's family, try not to let the divorce ruin the relationship. I had become very good friends with my wife's brother, and I wanted to remain friends. It took some time, but he came to understand that just because I couldn't live with his sister didn't mean that he and I couldn't get along.

—*GREG DEVRIES*
POLAND, OHIO
💔 💔9Y

. . . .

THE SUPPORT I FOUND in the days and months afterwards was from my family and a local church I found while soul-searching. I can't tell you how critical it is to not hole yourself up in your room and wallow in your own misery; it's important to find people who share your goals and want the same happiness that you want.

—*ALEX C. SCHAEFER*
BROOKFIELD, WISCONSIN
💔5Y 💔2Y

SEPARATION STATS

The Binuclear Family Study has found that one year after their divorce, 50 percent of couples had amicable relationships.

AT THE END OF MY MARRIAGE, I left most of our friends, except for my best friend. I didn't go to any of the usual summer parties that year or socialize much with anybody. I felt that because I was the one who left, I should give my spouse the opportunity to get support from our social circle. I also wasn't feeling particularly social. I just wanted to be by myself and heal.

—*PAMELA*
PHILADELPHIA, PENNSYLVANIA
18Y   15Y

MY PARENTS WERE AGAINST my divorce. Afterwards they saw the benefit of it; I was markedly happier and healthier. They hadn't realized it was the bad marriage making me sick, tired, and depressed until I was out of it.

—*KARIN TARPLEY*
SEATTLE, WASHINGTON
4Y   5Y

TRUST YOUR INTUITION and don't let other people dictate to you how you should feel or what you should do. If anyone judges you, just remind them that they didn't live with your spouse, and they don't know the whole story. It's none of their business anyway.

—*LESLIE YOUNG*
TACOMA, WASHINGTON
7Y   1Y

DON'T TRY TO SET ME UP with some guy you know from work. You have no idea what someone you work with is really like. Ted Bundy probably had some girl at work trying to set him up with some divorcée.

—*SANDRA FONKOUA*
SILVER SPRING, MARYLAND
1Y   6Y

Litigating Your Love: Lawyers, Legalities, and You

There aren't thousands of lawyer jokes for nothing. Then again, there aren't lawyers for nothing. For some people, dealing with a lawyer at such a difficult time is the icing on the now-rotten wedding cake. For others, it's the lawyers who help them through. Here are some tips for picking the right attorney for you, dealing with mediation, or navigating legal waters on your own.

BE AMICABLE. Even though you're divorcing, try to maintain open lines of communication. You may not get along, but it could be a huge financial mess for both of you if you don't work together. Arguments require lawyers, and lawyers cost money.

—M.R.
HELLERTOWN, PENNSYLVANIA
💔2Y 💔 💔1.5Y

DON'T GET MAD, GET EVEN. REVENGE LASTS MUCH, MUCH LONGER THAN HATE.

—MITZI SNYDER
ZELIENOPLE, PENNSYLVANIA
💔17Y 💔28Y

KNOWLEDGE IS POWER. Know your opponent. Act, do not react. Take the offensive, not the defensive. Realize your strength and trust yourself.

> —EVE CARTWRIGHT
> NEEDHAM, MASSACHUSETTS
> 5Y 7Y

. . . .

IF YOU DON'T HAVE A PRENUPTIAL agreement, get a great divorce lawyer. It's worth the fees—my friend's ex-wife took the house, the kids, and even the dog.

> —DAVID

. . . .

SIT DOWN WITH A MEDIATOR before meeting with your attorneys. You have to see a mediator anyway before getting divorced, so why not do it first? Lawyers are only out for one thing: to make money. If you and your soon-to-be-ex are getting along, they lose. My ex-wife and I could've saved $8,000 if we'd worked out our differences with a mediator beforehand. Instead, we wasted a ton of time and money arguing about everything in front of our lawyers—from the house, to the custody arrangements, and the vehicles.

> —DOUGLAS MUTKA
> LITTLETON, COLORADO
> 10Y 6Y

. . . .

YOU DON'T WANT TO PICK A LAWYER who is a friend to both of you. In a small town, that's hard to avoid. My husband chose a friend of ours for the divorce, and I was really bitter about that. Find someone out of town, or a person you both dislike, if you live in a small community.

> —J.C.
> WICHITA, KANSAS

The best lawyer I found happened to be a woman and a mother.

—HANK
SAN JOSE,
COSTA RICA
7Y   6Y
4Y

THE FISHERMAN AND HIS WIFE

I worked as a legal assistant to a divorce attorney: If there is one thing I learned, it's that revenge is very expensive. We had a client who was an airline pilot. He was in his 60s and was on his third wife, a flight attendant he'd been married to for 10 years. There was no big house, but they had a nice condo, and a very big yacht. He wanted the boat. He said it was for his business selling boats. He used it as a model. She just wanted to sell the yacht. Meanwhile, she moved out of the condo, he moved out of the condo, and it sat there empty. He refused to do the paperwork on the condo until she relinquished any interest in the boat. In the end, despite repeated warnings, the condo ended up in foreclosure and was repossessed. They lost it completely and not only ended up without any benefit from the property, but they trashed their credit record.

—A.T.
ARLINGTON, MASSACHUSETTS

MY WIFE AND I AGREED on the divorce, and we agreed completely on how we would divide our things. We had only been married three years, so it was pretty easy to say I'd keep what I brought and she'd keep what she'd brought. We had everything written out on eight pages of paper. It was very friendly. Then she went to a lawyer, and it all fell apart. The lawyer looked at the papers and told her she could get much more than that. That was the end of the friendliness.

—Z.
HELLERTOWN, PENNSYLVANIA
4Y

HEAD LINES
Best Advice and Top Tips

- A mediator can be a more amicable—and cheaper—alternative to a divorce lawyer.

- No matter how cordial you and your spouse may be during a divorce, it is still a good idea to have a lawyer whose sole purpose is to look out for you.

- Even if you and your spouse are able to agree on financial issues and custody arrangements without a lawyer, be sure to get everything in writing.

- The best approach to finding a good lawyer is to get personal recommendations from friends.

- The party who files the divorce papers ends up spending much more money than the party who is served.

I HAD A REALLY GOOD LAWYER: She was awesome. She was sympathetic to my story and gave me confidence it would be over quickly. She said, "With what I see here, we can wrap this up in 30 days." That would have been true if we'd been dealing with a reasonable person: It took a full year before we got in front of a judge. When it finally went down, the judge gave me more than I had asked for in terms of the split. She gave me $10,000 alimony that I hadn't asked for, and she gave my ex a lecture for dragging it out to this point, that he couldn't always have all he wanted in life. That was awesome.

—*Anonymous*
Atlanta, Georgia
3Y 8Y

WE BOTH WANTED IT TO BE as amicable as possible. We didn't want to be litigious or go to court. But that didn't mean I didn't need an attorney. No matter how fair my husband and I were trying to be, I needed someone looking out for me—period.

—*JENNIFER*
LAS VEGAS, NEVADA
💔8Y 💔 💔20Y

• • • • • • • •

Get yourself a good pen. There are so many forms that you will end up filling out. You won't believe how many times you sign your name before it's all over.

—*DONALD WINKLE*
ELLSWORTH, OHIO
💔6Y 💔6Y

• • • • • • • •

GET IN TOUCH WITH THE VERY BEST legal counsel, preferably by recommendation. Don't just open the yellow pages and pick someone out. I was referred by a friend to someone who was very sympathetic and easy to talk to; very respectful. And that was important. A woman, particularly, needs to be sure she relates to the person very well. The attorney will serve as a caretaker as well as a legal counselor. It needs to be someone who will hold your hand.

—*ANONYMOUS*
GREENWICH, CONNECTICUT
💔45Y 💔1Y

TIPS ON FINDING AND WORKING WITH A DIVORCE LAWYER

1. The Internet is not a good place to find a lawyer.

2. Recommendations from friends are helpful.

3. Calling your local bar association is also an excellent way to get started.

4. It's important to keep in close contact with the lawyer.

5. Feel free to ask where they are in the process and to supply them with new information as soon as you receive it.

6. Let the lawyer know you are willing to do errands, make copies, or do research at the courthouse, and see if he or she is open to this idea. It can help keep your costs down.

Taking a proactive part in the legal process rather than just sitting back and expecting the lawyer to do everything is ultimately a much more empowering approach to the divorce process.

—MARGARET
BOULDER, COLORADO
13Y 14Y

MY HUSBAND WAS A LAWYER, and when I told him I wanted a divorce, he volunteered to draw up all the papers himself. I was naïve and over-whelmed; it never occurred to me this might be a bad idea . . . and it was actually a terrible idea! My husband, a successful lawyer who had never lost in court, wasn't about to lose this divorce. In the papers he drew up, he got the house, the Audi, half the Waterford crystal and the golden retriever. I ended up with the tent, the used car, and the dachshund. I also got my freedom. In the end, that turned out to be enough, but if I had it to do over again, I definitely would get my own attorney.

> —*A.F.*
> *PHILADELPHIA, PENNSYLVANIA*
> 6Y 20Y

• • • • • • • •

WHEN DIVORCING SOMEONE in the military, you need an attorney with expertise in this area, as the laws that apply are different from those for a civilian divorce. I found this out the hard way. My husband was a Marine, but I never really thought that divorcing a Marine would be any different from divorcing a cab driver. Boy, was I wrong. I did find out that there are many lawyers out there that specialize in this. I just wish I had known that ahead of time.

> —*DENISE LABATOS*
> *YOUNGSTOWN, PENNSYLVANIA*
> 24Y 6Y

• • • • • • • •

ATTORNEYS HAVE NO FINANCIAL BACKGROUND at all and most are bad at managing their own money. Do not rely on your attorney to get the best settlement for you. You need a financial advisor.

> —*MAGGIE*
> *BROOKLINE, MASSACHUSETTS*
> 5Y 2Y 2Y

AGREE AND SAVE

Compared with tens of thousands of dollars for litigation, the average cost for mediation is only $600 to $1,000.

Why do
people behave
like such
babies when
they're getting
divorced?
Grow up
already, and
behave like
adults.

—*J.B.*
SAN FRANCISCO,
CALIFORNIA
3Y 5Y

MY WIFE AND I HAD A MUTUAL FRIEND who was a divorce attorney. We both ran to him and asked him to represent us through the split. He told us both no. We were both pissed at him. After it was all over, though, I came to understand his decision. Whichever of us he had chosen, the other would never have spoken to him again. I had just lost my wife, but at least I retained him as my friend, and at that time I needed all the friends I could get.

> —*GEORGE RAPSO*
> *GIRARD, OHIO*
> *8Y 23Y*

• • • • • • • •

MAKE SURE THAT *YOU* FILE the divorce papers with the county! My husband had agreed to file the divorce papers, but I found out four months later that he had never filed them; we were still married! He knew that we were still married, but I spent those months assuming that we were divorced. When I found out, I immediately filed those papers myself!

> —*INGELA KOPONEN*
> *SWEDEN*
> *20Y 14Y*

• • • • • • • •

IF YOU KNOW IT'S GOING to go smoothly, you don't need an expensive "shark" lawyer. You can use your money for something else. I picked a cheap lawyer because I knew it wasn't going to be a big battle. We didn't have a lot of stuff to fight over. We didn't own a house. We had separate bank accounts. All I wanted was our twins and for the whole ordeal to be over as easily as possible. We came up with an amount for child support. He agreed. It was cut-and-dried.

> —*DELLA D.*
> *BRIDGEPORT, NEW YORK*

GET A MEDIATOR, or at least a lawyer with a mediation service attached. Lawyers often inflame situations; they'll show you exactly why you should be upset. Any divorce is going to involve compromise, and a mediator can help with that.

> —*ANONYMOUS*
> *AMHERST, MASSACHUSETTS*

IF YOU CAN GET THROUGH THE PROCESS without hiring lawyers, you are better off. My friend hired one for her divorce, and it sucked so much money out of the family fund that by the time it was over, there was no money left to fight over.

> —*JENNY*
> *SAN FRANCISCO, CALIFORNIA*

READ THE FINE PRINT

When I received my divorce papers from the friendly sheriff, I quickly disputed many of the details that my ex-husband offered in the agreement, then sent them on their merry way via FedEx. However, because I didn't realize I had to send in money along with my response, and I had no legal counsel to advise me, a $103 fee went unpaid. My husband and his trusty lawyer realized this and divorced me four days early on a default, without my presence in the courtroom. The new decree gave all of the assets to my ex-husband. The original document, offering to split our assets, was no longer honored. My ex also gave me an additional $11,000 in debt, to which a judge agreed. So ladies, please make sure that all fees are paid! Take the initiative. Or better yet, get an attorney if you can afford one.

> —*JANE DEBATTY*
> *DENVER, COLORADO*
> 💔 6M

NO MATTER HOW TIRED YOU ARE, how depressed, how scared, get a good lawyer and make sure you get what you and your children need. Just as there's no reason to be greedy, there's no reason to be naïve. If you can't come to a reasonable compromise without giving up everything, assume the other person is playing you and treat them as hostile.

—*R.F.*
TEL AVIV, ISRAEL
💔*9Y* 💔*4Y*

· · · · · · · ·

❝ Words of wisdom: If you ever get divorced, be sure to pick your lawyer better than you picked your husband! ❞

—*LYNNE WATSON*
PHILADELPHIA, PENNSYLVANIA
💔*8Y* 💔*6Y*

· · · · · · · ·

I DIDN'T BOTHER WITH AN ATTORNEY. We were able to arrange custody, visitation and support, and I didn't care enough about the property to fight over dividing it. I would recommend that other people get lawyers, though, just to make sure they're covered. There are a few provisions that I would have liked to have in the divorce decree (such as a prohibition against overnight guests of the opposite sex when our daughter is present). An attorney might have thought of them when I didn't.

—*DAVID LODGE*
OKLAHOMA CITY, OKLAHOMA
💔*6Y* 💔*1Y*

AFTER THE DIVORCE, if one parent moves away from the other parent, the court may find that the parent who moved must pay for visitation travel expenses. If both parents have agreed to the move, then the court may find that both parties must share in the cost of transportation. I just wanted to get as far from my ex-wife as I could, but then I found out that I'd have to pay to transport her to where the kids and I were living: That was reason enough for me to stay put.

—*BRANDON BUCKLEY*
YOUNGSTOWN, PENNSYLVANIA
15Y 6Y

• • • • • • • •

GET EVERYTHING IN WRITING with your lawyer; look over everything. I didn't, and my lawyer jerked me over. He said he needed $1,000. I gave it to him. Then he said he needed $1,000 more for something else. It's a very emotional time. You're like, "I just want it over with. Just give me the divorce." So, you just slap the money over to him. Be careful.

—*DEBBIE L.*
CAMILLUS, NEW YORK
* 12Y*

• • • • • • • • •

I WANTED TO HAVE A PARTICULAR LAWYER whom I respected a lot. My wife didn't want to use that lawyer, because she cost a lot. She wanted to go through a mediator, but I said there was nothing to mediate. I wasn't willing to not have a lawyer, and I told her it wasn't a good idea for her either. But that was her choice. Ultimately, she allowed my lawyer to handle all the paperwork, and she agreed to pay for part of the cost.

—*J.S.*
WYNDMOOR, PENNSYLVANIA
20Y 1Y

The best advice I got from a lawyer: Assume that you are being tape-recorded when you are speaking with your spouse or your spouse's attorney.

—*B.D.*
STUTTGART,
GERMANY
7Y 4Y

DIVORCE NOIR

When we wanted a divorce, we thought it would be too expensive and time-consuming to get it in California. Since we'd been married in Nevada, we thought it would be easier to get divorced there. We went to Reno and looked through the yellow pages, but we found out you're supposed to reside in the state for at least three months. On one phone call, the woman seemed to say she knew of some way around it, so we went to her shop. It was in the middle of nowhere, and it was a divorce/bail-bond shop! The woman said, "There's somebody waiting for you," and sent us through some back door. There was a guy there we'd never seen before who said, "Yeah, I recognize you. You're my neighbors  from such-and-such street." He gave us an address and asked for $50. That seemed too cheap to us, so we gave him $100. Back out front, the woman gave us a place to get a mailbox number, and said they could backdate it three months.

The whole thing was like a cheesy B-movie; so surreal. We wrote ourselves a postcard for proof. Afterwards, we were just hoping the divorce would go through and be legal. It did, and it was a whole lot cheaper than it would have been in California!

—*Kammy T.*
San Francisco, California
💔3y 💔13y

WE ATTEMPTED MEDIATION FIRST. That failed because he tried to screw me out of half of his retirement pension, which I was entitled to. I got tired of his abusive nature and of always defending myself, so I asked around as to who was the best attorney in town.

—*CELIA*
OKLAHOMA CITY, OKLAHOMA
20Y 4Y

OVERLY OPTIMISTIC?

Only five percent of married couples have prenuptial agreements.

MY HUSBAND AND I AVOIDED getting a divorce for years after we broke up because of the cost and frustration of dealing with lawyers. And when we finally did it, it was awful. Things we had always dealt with well, in terms of support and custody, became sore points. His lawyer advised him that he could get away with less child support; my lawyer told me I was getting ripped off. We ended up angry all over again. My advice is to not get married, so you don't have to deal with all that stuff if it ends.

—*BRENDA*
CHARLESTON, WEST VIRGINIA
24Y 8Y

THE DIVORCE PROCESS IN CHICAGO is every bit as corrupt as City Hall. The judges who were once lawyers only care about the lawyers getting paid. Truth, fairness, and justice have no place within the four walls of a courtroom. Lawyers drain you of all your money and then drop your case; it happened to both me and my ex-wife during the process.

—*G.D.*
CHICAGO, ILLINOIS
17Y 1Y

REMEMBER, THE ATTORNEY WORKS FOR YOU! He or she is there to advise you, but the final decision is yours, and it is the attorney's job to fight for your decision, right or wrong. I have been told by an attorney, "I have never been told what to do, and I won't allow you to dictate to me now," even though I pay his fees.

—*ANONYMOUS*
INDIANAPOLIS, INDIANA
💔10Y 💔8Y

• • • • • • • •

I COULD HAVE SAVED MYSELF a lot of money in legal fees by doing some of the legwork myself. Ask your lawyer if there are petitions that you can file or papers that you can have a friend serve. Make phone calls or retrieve documents for your lawyer when you can. You don't have to be a helpless bystander throughout the process. And getting your hands dirty will make you feel better about it. But you have to be proactive about this stuff. Don't expect your lawyer to bring it up.

—*BETSY ANDERSEN*
CANFIELD, OHIO
💔 💔8Y

• • • • • • • •

THE STATE WHERE WE LIVED had pro se divorce; you do the paperwork and represent yourself in court. There has to be mutual agreement between the two parties and no children involved. You have to toss a coin to see who is going to file and who is going to be served. The man I was divorcing picked me up on the way to the courthouse; we went together. There were no lawyers, just a judge. The judge banged his gavel, and then we went out to breakfast together.

—*SALLY*
VERONA, VIRGINIA
💔 💔4Y

I COULDN'T STAND MY ATTORNEY, but he was funny. At the end of the whole process, he pulled me aside and told me this joke. "What do you call 1,000 divorce attorneys at the bottom of the sea?" "A good start." I laughed so hard my sides hurt. He was despicable, but at least he had a great sense of humor.

—R.A.
CALLA, OHIO
4Y 1Y

DO NOT THINK THAT IF YOU DON'T ANSWER the divorce papers or cooperate, your spouse will not be able to divorce you. In fact, your spouse might be able to not only get a divorce, but get everything he asks for.

—ANONYMOUS
STRUTHERS, OHIO
12Y 7Y

CUSTODY OF KIDS

Don't make custody of the kids about anything other than the children. You have to be very objective. It was hard for me to come to the decision of joint custody, because I wanted control of how my child was raised; I wanted to be the only influence. I thought my influence would be the best for him and I did not like the idea of never being able to live more than 100 miles from my ex, which limited my choices. I am glad I came to the decision of joint custody because our son will know we both want him and love him. Our son spends a week at a time with each of us and we both have the option to have him one night in the middle of the week, so we don't have to miss him too much. He is such a happy, well-adjusted kid.

—ALEXIS
KNOXVILLE, TENNESSEE
5Y 2Y

You really
don't need a
lawyer. Many
courts have
a clerk who
can tell you
what you need
to do.

—*HANK*
SAN JOSE,
COSTA RICA
🖤7Y 🖤 🖤6Y
🖤 🖤4Y

I DOWNLOADED A MARITAL separation agreement
from the Internet, and we hammered it out on a
particularly long day. It was seven hours of arguing about this and that, but we finally came to an
agreement and had it notarized. I have an uncle
who's a lawyer, and he looked it over to make sure
that it was legally sound. My ex paid for a lawyer
to file an uncontested divorce and the agreement
was incorporated into the divorce decree.

—*L.Q.*
HAMPTON ROADS, VIRGINIA
🖤14Y 🖤2M

. . . .

I RECOMMEND PREPAID LEGAL PLANS. They are an
affordable way to have legal access. I pay a monthly
fee for legal service. I had some phone conversa-
tions with my attorney and ran the documents past
her. It was helpful to be able to consult an attorney
to make sure all the legal paperwork was taken
care of properly, and to understand the process.

—*ALLEN R. PYLE*
HILLSDALE, MICHIGAN
🖤9Y 🖤8M

. . . .

I FOUND MY ATTORNEY in the yellow pages: I
would not recommend him to anyone. He knew
my husband was a deadbeat, but he just didn't
really seem to care about the situation. I did get
sole custody of my daughter, but that was
because I asked for it and my ex didn't fight me
on it. If you are planning to get divorced, ask
friends or colleagues for references. Or the best
thing to do is call another attorney and ask them
who they would want for their divorce attorney.
If you make enough phone calls, the same name
will keep coming up.

—*B.D.*
STUTTGART, GERMANY
🖤7Y 🖤4Y

THINK FINANCIALLY AND ACT LEGALLY. Don't expect the legal system to take care of you. The future is in your hands, not the court's. The legal system is not designed to help you with your finances once the divorce is granted. You will have to make all the decisions about your financial future. The legal process of divorce is something you will live through, but the financial reality is what you will have to live with for the rest of your life.

> —V.W.
> NEWPORT BEACH, CALIFORNIA
> 💔2Y 💔6Y

• • • • • • • •

> Brace yourself. Our divorce has been a bigger nightmare than the actual marriage. 🙶
>
> —BONNIE RUSSELL
> DEL MAR, CALIFORNIA
> 💔4Y 💔 💔4Y

• • • • • • • •

WE HAD ATTORNEYS AT FIRST, and we would fight over the smallest things, like who got CDs or fine china. Finally we decided to see a mediator who is a neutral party that is not representing either person. She went over our finances and worked out an equitable arrangement. We decided to keep his attorney for filing purposes; he took the mediated agreement and filed it for us. And mediation cost only $200, as opposed to a couple of grand for attorneys. The best thing about it is that neither of us hated the other and we respected each other afterwards. Amazingly, the day we had to appear in court together we actually had lunch afterwards.

> —SARAH
> RALEIGH, NORTH CAROLINA
> 💔7Y 💔

KNOW WHERE YOUR LAWYER STANDS on political and family issues before you hire him. I found out that my original lawyer was a father's rights advocate—after he worked out some deals with my ex-husband's lawyer on an issue that had already been decided in my favor. This was not exactly the person I needed on my side while I was fighting to keep sole custody of my child.

　　　　　—JAMIE TEAL
　　　　　NATICK, MASSACHUSETTS
　　　　　💔3Y 💔 💔3Y

⋆ ⋆ ⋆ ⋆ ⋆ ⋆ ⋆ ⋆

YOUR ATTORNEY WILL TRY to talk you into asking for more or not giving as much; that is their job. So if you and your spouse outlined a basic settlement before you hired attorneys, just stick to your guns. If possible, use only one attorney.

　　　　　—ALEXIS
　　　　　KNOXVILLE, TENNESSEE
　　　　　💔5Y 💔2Y

⋆ ⋆ ⋆ ⋆ ⋆ ⋆ ⋆ ⋆

IF BOTH YOU AND YOUR HUSBAND are thinking about getting a divorce, hold out and wait for him to file: It will save you a ton of money. Whoever actually files for divorce ends up paying much more than the other party. I only paid about $65, and I know he paid much more than that.

　　　　　—VAL TOSEKI
　　　　　CANFIELD, OHIO
　　　　　💔9Y 💔26Y

THE WORST THING TO HEAR #1

"Do you have a good lawyer?" It infuriates me. This is support from friends and family? Give me a break.

　　—A.C.
　　NEW YORK, NEW YORK
　　💔12Y 💔1Y

WOMEN, MAKE SURE you are set up for the long haul. Make sure to get some of the 401k, and make sure that he can't change the beneficiary on his life insurance policy. Even if you have to make the premiums, as long as you have this policy in effect, you will be paid before any other future wife. You are not being evil or nasty; you are protecting yourself. Do not let anyone say otherwise.

> —*ANONYMOUS*
> *EDMONDS, WASHINGTON*
> 16Y 1Y

SPLIT-UP STAT

How much does a divorce lawyer cost? Between $50 and $450 per hour.

MY DIVORCE ATTORNEY WAS a friend of my sister. Some years later, when I understood what a mess he had made of my divorce, I regretted that decision. My only comfort was in knowing that he was disbarred a few years later, so he isn't messing up other divorces! My second divorce was a do-it-yourself. Since we had no kids together and I took everything I wanted when I left, it was a no-brainer. All of the necessary forms are available through the county Web site.

> —*DIANE EVANS*
> *RENTON, WASHINGTON*
> 8Y 6Y 13Y

WE SHARED A LAWYER and made a list of what we each wanted. I basically let her draw up the list and respected her desires. We sold the house and split the proceeds. There was never a question of alimony as we both have always worked and child support is determined by the state. I think in the end it cost about $2,500. We share joint custody of our son. Although he lives with my ex-wife, I have extremely liberal visitation.

> —*KYLE*
> *FAIRFIELD, CONNECTICUT*
> 13Y 7Y

Check e-mail
carefully
before sending
it, because
e-mails can be
used in divorce
cases. The less
emotional you
are, the better.

—*ANONYMOUS*
EDMONDS,
WASHINGTON
💔16Y 💔1Y

LET THE LAWYERS HANDLE CONTACT with the
spouse. If you're lucky, your ex will leave the
country. Mine did, and the whole thing seems
less-than-real to me five years later.

> —*L.A.*
> *CHICAGO, ILLINOIS*
> 💔2Y 💔6Y

· · · · · · · ·

TAKE YOUR DIGNITY and self-respect with you. I was
determined to do this, so I had my lawyer draw up
divorce papers on grounds of adultery. I was not
going to take "irreconcilable differences" as a reason for the dissolution of my marriage. I prevailed!

> —*KATRINA PIPASTS*
> *PARK RIDGE, ILLINOIS*
> 💔17Y 💔3Y

· · · · · · · ·

LEGAL HASSLES SIMILAR to *The War of the Roses*
lasted for five years with us, costing thousands of
dollars, five years of my life, and loss of self-
respect. Luckily I had jewelry to sell to pay for
the attorney's fees.

> —*GEORGENE*
> *CRYSTAL BEACH, FLORIDA*
> 💔7Y 💔 💔13Y 💔 💔3Y

· · · · · · · ·

AFTER WAITING MY HUSBAND OUT and disabusing
him of the idea that he would be getting alimony
from me, we filed the papers ourselves just to
get it over with. The only thing I wanted from my
marriage was what I came into the marriage with.

> —*J.M. CORNWELL*
> *TABERNASH, COLORADO*
> 💔13Y 💔22Y

What's Mine Is Mine: Splitting Finances and Property

*W*hether *or not you choose to deal with attorneys, you* will *deal with dividing your stuff—from those retro CDs you used to play over your romantic dinners (ha!), to the cash in your checking account. How to decide what to fight for, and what to leave behind? Read what others did.*

MY HUSBAND AND I HAD a lot of stuff between us, but our biggest argument was over a Joni Mitchell tape; we both refused to give it up. Somehow, it symbolized our entire breakup. In the end, I got the tape, but it was a hollow victory. I was never able to listen to it again.

—*A.F.*
PHILADELPHIA, PENNSYLVANIA
💔*6Y* 💔*20Y*

BE SELFISH EMOTIONALLY. BE GENEROUS FINANCIALLY.

—*M.T.*
CHICAGO, ILLINOIS

HEAD LINES
Best Advice and Top Tips

- Try not to get wrapped up in petty disputes over possessions.
- If you don't take something you want when you move out, you are unlikely to get it later.
- Protect yourself: Close joint accounts and cut up joint credit cards immediately.
- When making a budget for your new life, don't factor in child support—if you get it, great; but it's best not to count on it.
- Keep in mind that if you are paying alimony, it will stop when your ex remarries.

Don't try to fleece the guy. My husband had the house before he was married; he had it after. Why would I want his house?

—ANONYMOUS
SAN ANTONIO,
TEXAS
🏠3Y 💔25Y

DON'T BE AFRAID TO TAKE what is rightfully yours. I sold my car to get a Firebird for my husband. The day I left him, I went out and I took the car with me: It was mine. He asked several times if he could borrow it. I said, "No."

—LISA K. MCDANIEL
SAN ANTONIO, TEXAS
🏠4Y 💔13Y

• • • • • • • •

STAY IN THE HOUSE! When my husband moved out, everything in the house was mine; at least, that's the way I thought about it. He may remember the dining room set was his, but he didn't remember about the sheets. You need to stay, because all the little things get left with you. If you move out, it's hard to come back and go through everything.

—ANONYMOUS
KANSAS CITY, MISSOURI
🏠 💔 🏠14Y

THERE IS A BENEFIT TO LIVING in a community property state. In California, everything gets split fifty-fifty. Knowing that, we just made a list and went through it. Her stuff prior to the marriage was hers; mine was mine; and the items we accumulated during the marriage were split up evenly. I think one of the ways we made it easy was that we waited about three months until all the initial emotions had subsided before we dealt with all the legal and financial stuff.

—*DANIEL H. AMINOFF*
ALEXANDRIA, VIRGINIA
6Y 4Y

. . . .

" Just take yourself out of the relationship in one piece if you can. All that other stuff can be replaced. "

—*MARIO ONCEY*
POLAND, OHIO
6Y 8Y

. . . .

MAKE SURE THAT YOUR NAME is not on something that you don't want to be responsible for. My ex took the car and the car payments. Later, he was selling the car but my name was still on the title. I had to go down to the courthouse at a certain time of day and it was a pain. I asked him, "What would have happened if I had moved to Massachusetts? Would you have been able to sell the car?"

—*CHRISTINE C. GODIN*
SAN ANTONIO, TEXAS
5Y 11Y

GET IT NOW OR REGRET IT LATER

The most difficult thing about my divorce was money. I handled the settlement agreement completely wrong. I didn't want a confrontation or anything to disturb the co-parenting of our child, I wasn't assertive enough to ask for what was reasonable, and I've regretted that for years. Money was one of the reasons our marriage didn't work, and my ex-husband still has huge money issues. He has contributed almost nothing to taking care of our son. But the worst thing was that when our son was ready to go to college and I called his father to ask what he could contribute, he said, "Nothing." I said to him, "Are you telling me that in all the years you've been working at well-paying jobs, you've never put any money aside for your son's college education?" His response was, "That is not a fair question." He simply refused to discuss it.

Bottom line: Stand up for yourself and get a divorce settlement that's what you and your children deserve, or you'll have a lot of years to wish that you had.

—Mariah
Toronto, Canada
5y 20y

BE WILLING—perhaps eager—to give away anything not among the essentials. Don't get greedy: We don't really need much of the junk we carry around. This may entail some battles with your own pride. Don't succumb to this; that just makes you feel petty. But don't go and make a sanctimonious martyr of yourself; that's just another way of succumbing to pride.

> —ARCH
> LONDONDERRY, VERMONT
> 18Y 1Y

• • • • • • • •

I REMEMBER STANDING in front of my ex-husband with two ladles in my hands—one with holes for draining, one without. I said, "Which one do you want?" He could never make up his mind about anything. Watching him torture himself over divvying up a couple of ladles reminded me of how much I wanted to be done with him—and cooking!

> —E.P.
> WEST STOCKBRIDGE, MASSACHUSETTS

• • • • • • • •

DO YOUR HOMEWORK before you file for divorce. Make sure there are no hidden monies and check your credit card slips to make sure they are not being used by your soon-to-be ex and his new significant other.

> —ANONYMOUS
> INDIANAPOLIS, INDIANA
> 10Y 8Y

• • • • • • • •

I STAYED AND KEPT THE HOUSE, the debts, the responsibility, and it nearly killed me. After eight years alone, I ended up filing for bankruptcy.

> —SARALYN
> CHICAGO, ILLINOIS
> 28Y 10Y

SPLIT-UP STAT

Following a divorce, a woman's standard of living decreases by 27 percent, while a man's standard of living increases by 10 percent.

TRY NOT TO MAKE SOMETHING already so personal more personal than it is. You can get back material things later. Your main focus should be getting things settled in as fair a manner as possible, and getting the hell out of there. Get on with your life. Don't cry too much if you don't get the dishes.

—*RAVEN*
TACOMA, WASHINGTON
2Y   2Y

"**Don't get hung up on money, even if it's a lot of money. Settle the financial stuff up front, and then get on with the more important things, like learning from your mistakes.**"

—*M.T.*
CHICAGO, ILLINOIS

 POSSESSION IS NINE-TENTHS of the law! I cannot stress this enough. I have lost almost everything I own because I did not take it with me when I left the house. My ex sold most of my stuff (like my snowmobile and bike) or he threw it away, and there is no proof, so it's just gone! Please, if you want to keep it, take it with you.

—*M.W.*
FORT MYERS, FLORIDA
12Y   1M

WE BOTH WANTED TO KEEP OUR DOG, so we decided to share custody. This was not an easy decision, but it's one that seemed to be fair. We tried different rotations and saw how she reacted. We realized that rotating weeks made sense for all of us. We worked it out so that the dog would join us on Friday afternoon. This way, we each had two weekends off a month to go out of town if we wanted.

—*MICHELLE*
TORONTO, ONTARIO
2Y 1Y

ONLY YOU AND YOUR EX KNOW your weak spots. Protect yourself as much as you can. My ex knew that my weak spot was my daughter and the still-born daughter we lost: She used that to hurt me the best way she could. She refused to give me pictures and lied in court, saying they were lost or destroyed. So if there are things in the house that you need or want, take them when you leave. You may never have a chance to get them again.

—*G.D.*
CHICAGO, ILLINOIS
17Y 1Y

Possessions shouldn't be divided equally; they should be divided as to who cares more about what.

—*ANONYMOUS*
BOULDER,
COLORADO
4Y 7Y

A FRIEND OF MINE who got divorced a couple years before I did told me to take my wife's pillow and hide it right before she moved out. He said there would be many nights after she was gone that I would have an overwhelming need to just hit something. He said instead of hitting and breaking something of mine, I could just wail away on her pillow and get all my frustration out. It worked.

—*BENNY TADFORD*
YOUNGSTOWN, OHIO
20Y 24Y

ONE THING TO INSIST ON TAKING WITH YOU

THE DOG. I figured I was going to need all the comforting I could get. I needed someone to occupy that other side of the bed for a while.

> —*M.S.*
> *CARNEGIE, PENNSYLVANIA*
> 20Y ♥ 7Y

. . . .

THE MICROWAVE. I knew absolutely nothing about cooking, so I needed the microwave so that I wouldn't starve. Anybody can throw a frozen meal in a microwave. Besides, it was a wedding gift from my sister, so why should my wife get it?

> —*B.G.*
> *PITTSBURGH, PENNSYLVANIA*
> 8Y 5Y

. . . .

THE HOUSE. Why? Because it's the most expensive thing to replace: End of story.

> —*J.J.*
> *BULGER, PENNSYLVANIA*
> 1Y 22Y 4Y

. . . .

THE COMPUTER, to get on those online dating sites and find a new girl. That's exactly how I found my second wife.

> —*P.S.*
> *CARNEGIE, PENNSYLVANIA*
> 7Y 7Y

. . . .

ART. We had bought a piece by a woman from New Orleans at an outsider-art gallery: a black Madonna all in glitter with a gold frame. It was the first thing I put in my new place.

> —*HAWLEY HUSSEY*
> *BROOKLYN, NEW YORK*
> ♥ 2Y

A SIGNED GLASS SCULPTURE that we had bought in Italy in lieu of an engagement ring. We litigated over it: I won.

—*BONNIE RUSSELL*
DEL MAR, CALIFORNIA
4Y 4Y

THE PETS. But then you have to hire a pet trainer to brainwash and deprogram them from all the stuff that your stupid wife taught them. My wife let me take the dog because it was really my dog in the first place. But she'd taught him to roll over whenever he wanted to go outside. After the divorce it drove me crazy to watch him do that, knowing that it was her idea. But I couldn't break him of it.

—*T.O.*
CANFIELD, OHIO
4Y 5Y

PHOTOS. Believe me, it might not seem important at the time, but there will come a day when you'll wish you fought harder for those baby pictures.

—*CHET YARO*
STRUTHERS, OHIO
19Y 8Y

JEWELRY. If you bought it for her, it's yours.

—*MERLE USHER*
POLAND, OHIO
12Y 4Y

MY COMIC BOOK COLLECTION, because I told her I'd sooner burn it than let her have it.

—*BARRY*
CHICAGO, ILLINOIS

WHEN YOU SELL THE HOUSE, don't tell the real estate agent that you are getting divorced, especially if it's a bitter divorce. That's because they'll let people know you're a motivated seller, and buyers will offer you less. You and your soon-to-be ex will both get more money if you present a united front to the agent.

When we were house-hunting ourselves, my wife and I had been encouraged to bid low on properties where the sellers were getting divorced, so we knew better when it was our turn to sell under the same circumstances.

> —J.K.
> LOS ANGELES, CALIFORNIA
> 2Y 7Y

• • • • • • • •

I AM A BIG FAN OF the prenuptial agreement; I guess most women are. It can really be your security blanket. My first husband had a super-good job and he insisted I sign the prenup before we got married. Looking back, it was probably better for me than for him. We had such a nasty divorce and he had friends in high places that might have made it hard for me to get anything at all out of him without the agreement. The way I look at it, it's better to get something out of the scumbag than nothing at all.

> —ANONYMOUS
> SOUTH BEND, INDIANA

• • • • • • • •

SIMPLE: I took the dog, he took the stereo. I took the living room furniture, he took the bed. It was really weird how that all worked out.

> —MARGARET STECK
> SEATTLE, WASHINGTON
> 4Y 7Y

WE DECIDED THAT if it was a gift from his family, he kept it. If it was a gift from my family, I kept it. Everything else we tried to divide up evenly. I got the bedroom suite in the master bedroom, he got the one in the guest room. Since the dishes were a gift from my family, I took them. I actually ended up buying him his first set of dishes.

> —*ELIZABETH*
> *SALISBURY, NORTH CAROLINA*
> 1Y 13Y

• • • • • • • •

HE TOOK WHAT HE WANTED and told me to deal with the rest. I didn't care: I just wanted him out of my house. Of course, if he took a dresser, the drawers just got emptied onto the floor. He didn't take much, and I was left to deal with quite a lot. Afterward, he wanted to come back and get things he missed the first time. I didn't allow it. He then tried to get his attorney to make me tally everything in the house and pay him half the value. My attorney told him to shove it, and I never heard another word about that.

> —*CELIA DUNBAR*
> *OKLAHOMA CITY, OKLAHOMA*
> 20Y 4Y

• • • • • • • •

DIVORCING COUPLES ATTACH their emotional worth to material goods—especially the more affluent couples. Their purchases are not just housekeeping objects, but memorabilia, art objects, and collectibles. It takes a third party to divide fairly. A disinterested party would be one's own attorney. Another option is to have a member of his family meet with a member of yours. Just like in death, people become greedy and need a disinterested party to step in.

> —*GEORGENE*
> *CRYSTAL BEACH, FLORIDA*
> 7Y 13Y 3Y

SPLIT-UP STAT

One-fifth of families filing for bankruptcy have recently been through a divorce.

YOU NEED TO GET SOMETHING for what you give up. It's common to hand over your assets if you feel guilty or want to expedite the painful process of separating, but you may regret some of your choices later. I told my ex that she could have our house. If I did it again, I would've gotten an appraisal and at least got some money in exchange for this.

—*DAVE*
GREENBELT, MARYLAND
8Y 1Y

Dividing our possessions was actually quite simple: I just threw his stuff out the door.

—*DEBBIE L.*
CAMILLUS,
NEW YORK
12Y

• • • • • • • •

DIVIDE THE ASSETS and furniture as soon as possible. Get it in writing with an attorney and sign it as soon as possible. The longer you wait, the more likely you will get to the anger phase of divorce and start arguing over things.

—*ALEXIS*
KNOXVILLE, TENNESSEE
5Y 2Y

• • • • • • • •

LOTS OF PEOPLE THINK THAT, when a couple gets divorced, the woman "takes the man to the bank." This is a myth. When my marriage ended, my ex-husband kept our house with the pool and spa, and he didn't have to pay one cent of child support, because I made slightly more money than he did.

—*DEBBIE REDDEN-BRUNELLO*
TEMECULA, CALIFORNIA
15Y 4Y

• • • • • • • •

IF YOU THINK YOU MAY GET A DIVORCE, don't run up the credit card. I didn't realize that once you are legally separated, the bills become yours, even if you're not divorced yet.

—*M.R.*
PLANO, TEXAS
2Y

WHEN FILING FOR ALIMONY, look at the pros and cons of getting one lump-sum payment as opposed to receiving weekly or monthly payments. A lump sum may enable you to get a good start on your new life. I found that getting the money up front allowed me to move on with my life and to put the matter behind me. I figured that getting a check each month would continually open those wounds.

—*ELLEN WAYNE*
BOARDMAN, OHIO
5Y 10Y

You can't let dividing up things get to you. It's just stuff. Happily for us, she didn't want my fishing pole, and I saw no use for the china. We each got what was important to us.

—*HAROLD JAFFE*
REDMOND, WASHINGTON
16Y 26Y

CUT UP YOUR JOINT CREDIT CARDS immediately and do whatever it takes to protect yourself. I didn't shut the account down right away because I needed the credit, but this was a mistake. Even though our divorce decree said that the credit-card debt was my ex-husband's responsibility, I ended up having to pay the bill when they couldn't find him.

—*LISA BARNSTROM*
SAN ANTONIO, TEXAS
4Y 16Y

WOMEN, YOU JUST HAVE TO BE RUTHLESS through the whole divorce process. It's really your last chance to get yourself some financial security for the rest of your life. You have to put all the good times in the past and look at your husband and his money as your key to future happiness. Take no prisoners, or you'll regret it later.

—*J.P.*
CRANBERRY TOWNSHIP, PENNSYLVANIA
❤26Y ❤3Y

• • • • • • • •

❝You have to think beyond the obvious. Upon unpacking in our separate houses, we realized that my husband had ended up with all the wine, and I ended up with all the wine openers. ❞

—*JANNY*
SANTA CRUZ, CALIFORNIA

• • • • • • • •

MAKE A BUDGET that does not include child support. If you happen to actually get your child support, it will seem like a bonus; if you don't, you'll have a plan. And remember, it takes women a long time to recover financially from a divorce. Don't beat yourself up for being broke.

—*M.L.E.*
SARATOGA SPRINGS, NEW YORK
❤12Y ❤5Y

FREEZE ACCOUNTS IF YOU NEED TO. Although all of our monetary assets were to be split fifty-fifty, I did not have any of our files that showed all of our assets. While contacting different mutual fund companies (primarily through memory), I found out that my ex started redeeming shares without my knowledge. I ended up freezing all of those that I knew of. Although that meant that I could not access my share of the assets, at least the assets were still there.

> —KATHY
> KENT, WASHINGTON
> ⚡8Y 💧5Y

• • • • • • • •

I WISH I HAD WORKED OUT a more concrete plan for my child support. I should have set up a legal arrangement, but we had been working very hard to make it amicable for my daughter. It never crossed my mind that he would try to punish me by keeping her child-support money from her. He was delinquent for four years. Make a concrete plan! And make sure the amount will increase as your child gets older and the cost of living increases.

> —C.L.
> SANDSTON, VIRGINIA
> 🧡 💧 🧡4Y

• • • • • • • •

SPLIT-UP STAT

73 percent of Americans name money as the number one factor that affects their stress level.

A FRIEND GAVE ME A TIP ONE TIME: If you're getting a divorce and you think she's going to be getting married again soon, pay her alimony because it will stop when she gets married. I knew my ex-wife would be getting married soon, so in our divorce I agreed to give her child support and alimony. The alimony stopped when she got married.

> —KEN D.
> ATLANTA, GEORGIA
> 🧡19Y 💧 🧡20Y

THE WORST THING TO HEAR #2

"It's time to make your alimony and child-support payment again."

—GREG FOX
FROSTBURG,
MARYLAND
♥14Y 💔7Y

IF YOU'RE THE MAN, there's nothing you can do when it comes to divorce. Your ex will try to take everything you have and won't stop until she gets it all.

—B.O.
IOWA CITY, IOWA
♥10Y 💔2Y

• • • • • • • •

DON'T MAKE YOUR DIVORCE a power struggle. When I moved out, my ex and I decided to donate some of our shared things to charity. This helped us not fight over the items and do something good in the process.

—CHRISTINE
STROUDSBURG, PENNSYLVANIA

• • • • • • • •

TRY TO BE DETACHED through the process and don't get angry or vindictive, regardless of what the other person does. You will come out ahead in the end—even if it means losing a lot of money and possessions.

—ALLEN R. PYLE
HILLSDALE, MICHIGAN
♥9Y 💔8M

• • • • • • • •

GET YOUR BUTT and your beloved possessions out of harm's way as quickly as possible. She will not hesitate to try to exact revenge by shattering a favorite item of yours: Don't give her the satisfaction.

—DAN SANTOS
GREEN TREE, PENNSYLVANIA
♥15Y 💔8Y

The Deed Is Done: First Steps in a New Life

*T*he papers are signed and filed: You're free. Now what? If you're like many, it's a time of mixed emotions—happiness, confusion, sadness, delirium. One thing is certain: No matter how you feel right now, your life is still unfolding. It's up to you to make the best of it. Here's how others took those first steps.

ALWAYS BRING A CLOSE, supportive friend with you on the day you go to court to finalize it. No matter how much you like your lawyer, you need a good, loving friend along for the drama/trauma.

—*EILEEN P.*
    WEST STOCKBRIDGE, MASSACHUSETTS

GET A PET. A DOG OR A CAT; EVEN A FISH WILL DO.

—*V.C.*
    COALBURG, OHIO
    ♥4Y ♥ ♥7Y

THE DAY MY DIVORCE BECAME FINAL was my 29th birthday. The guy I was seeing at the time threw me a party at an Italian restaurant. There were 15 people and a lot of red wine.

—*ANONYMOUS*
ATLANTA, GEORGIA
3Y 8Y

• • • • • • • •

AFTER THE DIVORCE WAS FILED, I remember standing in the middle of my apartment: For the first time in my entire life, I was living alone. I decided to make a grilled cheese sandwich right then and eat it. It sounds silly, but being able to do something only for myself was a completely novel feeling. For years I had been thinking of someone else before myself at all times. It was fantastic.

—*SARAH*
SEATTLE, WASHINGTON
5Y 4Y

• • • • • • • •

MY WIFE BROUGHT THE PAPERS in the house and said, "Here you go." I signed and said, "Thanks, see ya." My mother, my girlfriend, and I went to a really expensive lunch after that. It was particularly important to do that because my ex was always complaining that I never took her to nice places.

—*EVAN*
ATLANTA, GEORGIA
1Y 5Y

• • • • • • • •

I WENT OUT AND BOUGHT myself an opal ring. For me, that was crazy. I don't even spend more than $25 on a pair of shoes, and I went out and spent more than $400 on a ring! But, at the time, it made me feel better.

—*ELIZABETH*
SALISBURY, NORTH CAROLINA
1Y 13Y

You have to take a deep breath and really think about your actions. Just give yourself an extra few minutes and think instead of acting impulsively.

—*ANONYMOUS*
CHICAGO, ILLINOIS
10Y 8Y
5Y

I DID TOO MANY CRAZY THINGS after it was final. My hormones were out of kilter, and I fell in love (lust) with the most unsuitable character—to this day I can't even remember his name. But I thought I would chuck it all for this man. There definitely is something to the chemistry of loss, and urgency to fill the void. I was too vulnerable and yet it was unrecognizable to me. People tried to tell me, but I refused to listen.

—*GEORGENE*
CRYSTAL BEACH, FLORIDA
💔7Y 💔 💔13Y 💔 💔3Y

⦿ ⦿ ⦿ ⦿ ⦿ ⦿ ⦿ ⦿ ⦿

Get a therapist: That's the first thing I did after getting divorced. I learned to let go of my anger and forgive. **"**

—*MARIA ISBELL*
AUSTIN, TEXAS
💔 💔6Y

⦿ ⦿ ⦿ ⦿ ⦿ ⦿ ⦿ ⦿ ⦿

I HAD DECIDED THAT AFTER MY DIVORCE, I was going to move to a new place, a city about 400 miles from where my husband and I had lived. I didn't have a job or know anyone there, which was just fine by me. I wanted a clean, fresh start. Right after I signed my divorce papers, I got in my car, which was loaded with my belongings, and started the drive north. I rolled all the windows down, turned up the stereo full blast, and started singing at the top of my lungs.

—*ANDREA*
PHILADELPHIA, PENNSYLVANIA
💔6Y 💔20Y

NO KIDDING

Divorce
is more
complicated
emotionally
than the death
of a spouse,
experts say.

I got my belly button pierced. It was something I had always wanted to do.

—*Marsha Poindexter*
Springfield, Missouri
💔15Y 💔1Y

I BECAME GOOD FRIENDS with my neighbor who had been married to a jerk for 25 years. So she and I shared a "divorce party." I was only 21 at the time, so I called a bunch of old high school friends and a lot of single guys. It was nice to be in touch with old friends whom I hadn't spoken to in a while— even though the circumstances were odd!

—*Shannon*
Las Vegas, Nevada
💔2Y 💔12Y

. . . .

YOU NEED TO TAKE SEVERAL MONTHS after the process is final to reevaluate and take care of yourself. Ask yourself how you negatively contributed to the relationship, and what you can improve about yourself. It is important to do this because problems in a relationship are never the fault of just one person, and if you survive one divorce and go on to another marriage without working on yourself, you will take your issues along with you to the next relationship, and likely be just as miserable. I've learned this lesson the hard way!

—*T.H.*
Barling, Arkansas
💔7Y 💔 💔12Y 💔 💔5Y

. . . .

WHAT DO YOU DO WITH your wedding band? In the book *The Pilot's Wife*, by Anita Shreve, the wife went to the spot where the plane had crashed and threw her wedding band into the water. That inspired me. After the divorce was finalized in court, I met my best girlfriend at a restaurant for lunch. We had two cosmos and we walked out to Lake Michigan. I threw my ring very ceremoniously into the lake. It was closure for me.

—*Katrina Pipasts*
Park Ridge, Illinois
💔17Y 💔3Y

HEAD LINES
Best Advice and Top Tips

- Do something for yourself: buy something extravagant, eat your favorite meal, or treat yourself to something else, as long as it's special.

- Celebrate with friends.

- Cry as much as you need to.

- Get a therapist or a pet—both will help you cope!

- Make a new start.

MY FRIENDS CELEBRATED my divorce with me at Top of the Hub, a romantic place with a fabulous panoramic view of Boston. They took me there because they thought it was good to celebrate what was ahead.

—*ANONYMOUS*
BOSTON, MASSACHUSETTS
3Y 1Y

I DIDN'T REALLY DO ANYTHING when my divorce became final. I felt relieved and I went and changed my driver's license to reflect my maiden name again. I was finally rid of him! I did get a little out of hand, acting like a 21-year-old and partying way too much, having one-night stands.

—*BECKIE*
SEATTLE, WASHINGTON
4Y 2Y

WHEN MY DIVORCE WAS FINAL, I cried a lot. But mostly I felt at peace. That's a sign I did the right thing. It was time to move on.
—*M.S.*
SEATTLE, WASHINGTON
💔*5Y* 💔*13Y*

· · · · · · · ·

"My divorce was finalized on Valentine's Day. I thought that was really amusing! When I got the paperwork, I jumped up and down yelling and screaming, 'Woo-hoo!' It was over, and I was very relieved."
—*KIM*
MINNEAPOLIS, MINNESOTA
💔*4Y* 💔*4Y*

· · · · · · · ·

AFTER MY DIVORCE WAS FINALIZED, I hung out with all the new friends I made from work and it felt good. My advice is to go with whatever feels right: If you feel like crying, do so; if you feel happy, express it!! There's no right or wrong way to feel during this process.
—*QUISQUEYA DE LA ROSA*
MARGATE, FLORIDA
💔*2Y* 💔*1Y*

ON THE DAY WE WENT TO SIGN the papers, we both started crying. The lawyer told us that he believed we still loved each other. He stepped out of the room to give us some time to think about whether we really wanted to go through with the divorce. It was sad, but we were not happy together. Sometimes things just don't work out: There is no need to be angry.

—*M.G.*
BELLEVILLE, ILLINOIS
♡3Y ♡ ♡1Y

• • • • • • • • •

I WAS TRAVELING TO DENVER for training the day I got a phone call from my attorney telling me the divorce was final. Fortunately, I was surrounded by a bunch of co-workers who'd known me for years. That night, we went out to the bars to drink and play pool. I think being away from home really helped make the transition smooth.

—*ANTHONY MANUEL*
KINDER, LOUISIANA
♡14Y ♡4Y

• • • • • • • • •

ALONE VS LONELY

Researchers sampled 8,600 adults, asking them if they felt lonely. Here's who said yes, by marital status:

4.6%	Married
14.5%	Never married
20.4%	Divorced
20.6%	Widowed
29.6%	Separated

KNOW THAT THE DESTINATION is always easier than the journey.

—*D.L.*
CHICAGO, ILLINOIS
💔*6Y* 💔*5Y*

THE LAST GOODBYE

We were the only couple showing up together for the divorce hearing, and neither of us had retained an attorney. Ours was the last motion before lunch. The hardest part of this process was leaving the courtroom. My ex-wife and I walked out into the mezzanine, spontaneously embraced each other with a bear hug, and blubbered harder than ever before. A moment later our judge passed by, robe flowing, looking back a moment, I'm sure thinking, "Hmmm, that's unusual." A trail of tears was made as we trudged a few blocks for food in Chinatown. It felt like the reverse of a Greek wedding. That metaphorical crystal chalice of hopes and dreams, visions I'd held until death do us part, was pulverized into countless shards. I think I would have preferred vivisection.

—*JOHN ANTHONY*
WASHINGTON, D.C.
💔*6Y* 💔*11Y*

Media Therapy: Movies, Books, Songs, and the Internet

The time will come when all your friends and your family are busy. You will be alone. And you will start thinking about your ex. This is not necessarily a bad thing; don't be afraid. But, if it gets to be too much, go where other people like you have gone to find relief: a romantic comedy on film, a hardcover weeper or a let-it-all-out blog. Read on for suggestions.

ANYTIME YOU FIND YOURSELF with nothing to do and nobody around, get on the computer and enter a chat room: There's always someone to talk to there.

—*K.J.*
LOWELLVILLE, OHIO
💔7Y 💔6Y

I GET A LITTLE ADRENALINE RUSH EVERY TIME I HEAR "I WILL SURVIVE."

—*MEG*
MARIETTA, GEORGIA
💔PENDING

FATHER OF THE BRIDE: I'm talking about the more recent one, starring Steve Martin as the father. I like it because it shows someone else suffering through a wedding. I also like it because I'm an old softy and it is a very romantic movie.

—*KURT HELBIG*
POLAND, OHIO
💔6Y 💔5Y

• • • • • • • •

A MOVIE THAT HELPED ME through is *Dumb & Dumber.* The movie is silly, but it's funny, and it forces me to remember how stupid and juvenile all men are.

—*DENISE ULRICH*
YOUNGSTOWN, OHIO
💔4Y 💔3Y

• • • • • • • •

THE WOODY ALLEN MOVIE *Play It Again, Sam* really hits the nail on the head about the way men tend to feel after going through a divorce. I must have watched that thing for a month straight after my divorce was final. It really helped me realize that I wasn't alone in what I was feeling.

—*RAY VINCET*
LAVALE, MARYLAND
💔19Y 💔13Y

• • • • • • • •

I HIGHLY RECOMMEND the book *The Passionate Marriage*, by Dr. David Schnarch, if you want inspirational words of hope and practical advice. Dr. Schnarch has been a marriage and sex counselor for over 20 years, and his approach is not the same old thing that people get from typical marriage counseling, as far as I can tell. This book makes a lot of sense.

—*RYAN YOUNG*
EL CERRITO, CALIFORNIA
💔5Y 💔4Y

I bought the entire series of *Sex and the City.*

—*KATRINA PIPASTS*
PARK RIDGE,
ILLINOIS
💔17Y 💔3Y

I LISTENED TO this country and western song called "Shut Up and Drive," by Chely Wright. There is a line in there that says something like, "This just isn't working for me, so shut up and drive."

—*KIM*
CHICAGO, ILLINOIS
💔17Y 💔10Y

• • • • • • • •

The weekend my ex-wife moved out, I rented the *Star Wars* trilogy. The apartment was empty, so I pulled out a mattress into the living room and watched the whole thing straight.

—*PATRICK REGAN*
CHICAGO, ILLINOIS
💔1Y 💔 💔3Y

• • • • • • • •

A TREMENDOUS HELP WAS reading the book *The Wisdom of Insecurity*, by Alan Watts. I had read it many years ago, but now it shed a new light on my newly found state of instability. It put a spiritual twist on my discomfort with suddenly being on my own.

—*CHRIS*
SAN DIEGO, CALIFORNIA

• • • • • • • •

WHAT BOOK HELPED ME through the hard times? The Bible.

—*ANONYMOUS*
CORRIGANVILLE, MARYLAND
💔2Y 💔2Y

CUTTING-EDGE RECOVERY

My first reaction was to join an Internet dating service. But most of the men were old, even if they were close to my age. I realized that at this point in my life, they simply *are* old. But they were just as frisky as they had been decades ago; that was not on my agenda. Eventually, I gave up and decided to create a blog.

A blog is a Web log and I have been getting a great response to mine from people all over who have been dealing with the same situation. It truly does help to know that others are feeling the same thing, because you can't feel so sorry for yourself when you hear their stories.

But . . . blogs are very public, so be careful what you put in them!

—*Anonymous*
Marietta, Georgia
💔 PENDING

CHECK OUT THE **1973** MOVIE *Divorce His—Divorce Hers*, with Elizabeth Taylor and Richard Burton. It really helped me to understand where my wife was coming from with some of the things she thought and felt.

> —*GEORGE ALLEN*
> *FROSTBURG, MARYLAND*
> ♥3Y ♥19Y

• • • • • • • •

FOR ANYONE WHO FELT really guilt-tripped by their spouse (as I did with a man who'd been raised Catholic), I'd highly recommend listening to Louden Wainwright III's song "Mr. Guilty." It's bitter and hilarious. I listened to it many times after my divorce, and it made me laugh every time.

> —*LORRAINE*
> *SEATTLE, WASHINGTON*

• • • • • • • •

IRRECONCILABLE DIFFERENCES with Drew Barrymore: If you have kids, I suggest you take a look at that one. Most parents are oblivious to what the kids are going through. This movie can be a real eye-opener.

> —*BARRY FITTERER*
> *CUMBERLAND, MARYLAND*
> ♥17Y ♥18Y

• • • • • • • •

THE WAR OF THE ROSES: I could relate to it. Like the couple in the movie, my husband and I kept trying to resurrect our marriage but without making any meaningful changes. If you don't learn from your history, you are doomed to repeat it. I loved Danny DeVito in it as an attorney: He was terrific. I still put that movie on sometimes when I'm feeling down.

> —*MARCY NUSSBAUMER*
> *NEW ALBANY, OHIO*
> ♥10Y ♥8Y

CIAO, BABY (TAKE ONE)

Warner Brothers sells a CD music compilation called *Divorce Songs for Her.* It includes songs titled "Someone Else's Trouble Now" and "You Can Have Him."

IT'S SO FUNNY NOW, but I would just sob every-time I heard Kenny Rogers' "Islands in the Stream." I remember sitting in a chair at my mom's house and crying for hours after that song came on the radio.

—*ANGIE*
OZARK, MISSOURI
🖤1Y 💔 🖤5Y

• • • • • • • •

"If they'd made a movie about Lorena Bobbitt, I'd have watched it 24 hours a day."

—*B.V.*
NORTH JACKSON, OHIO
🖤6Y 💔3Y

• • • • • • • •

ANY MOVIE WITH KATHERINE HEPBURN in it: *Morning Glory* or *Stage Door,* both from the 1930s, are terrific. She was such a strong role model for women. My daughter's middle name is Katherine, for her. Also, movies with Meg Ryan, like *When Harry Met Sally* or *You've Got Mail,* are cute, romantic movies that don't hurt after a divorce. They make you feel that love is possible again.

—*DANA*
ANNISTON, ALABAMA
🖤6Y 💔 🖤1Y

• • • • • • • •

WHAT BOOK HELPED ME through the hard times? My diary.

—*TERRY HARRINGTON*
CUMBERLAND, MARYLAND
🖤7Y 💔10Y

THERE WAS ONE PERSON who really helped me see the light. She was the only person who truly felt the same way that I did, and still do. Although she is a fictional character, I believe that she is based on a true soul. Charlotte York (Kristen Davis's character on *Sex and the City*) still believes in true love: Her incessant optimism and love affair with love gave me insight and hope.

—*STACEY SAMUELS*
CHICAGO, ILLINOIS
💔2Y 💔2Y

• • • • • • • •

SOMETHING'S GOTTA GIVE is a great movie after or during your divorce because it helps you see that love is possible again. Neither character ever thought they'd fall in love again. They are older— so it's not a romantic comedy with young people falling in love for the first time. It's also great for showing that you can have a good relationship with your ex, since Diane Keaton's character does.

—*ALEXIS*
KNOXVILLE, TENNESSEE
💔5Y 💔2Y

• • • • • • • •

THE MOVIE VERSION OF *The World According to Garp* has a big divorce scene in it. In the movie, he discovered his wife was having an affair, and it accurately represented a lot of the emotions, especially his sense of outrage. Also, I watched *American Beauty* while I was going through my divorce. It represented the gamut of emotions I felt—the woman having an affair and Kevin Spacey's character rediscovering freedom, I related to that very strongly.

—*EVAN*
ATLANTA, GEORGIA
💔1Y 💔5Y

CIAO, BABY (TAKE TWO)

Warner Brothers sells a CD music compilation called *Divorce Songs for Him.* It includes songs titled "Here's a Quarter: Call Someone Who Cares" and "Party Time."

I can only
recall that I
listened to
Celine Dion
a lot.

—*GEORGENE*
CRYSTAL BEACH,
FLORIDA
💔7Y 💔 💔13Y
💔 💔3Y

MY ONLINE DIVORCE-SUPPORT GROUP got me
through the hardest time of my life. I also met a
male friend in that support group who was so
sweet to me that I realized that this is how it
should always have been. I realized what I was
missing in my own marriage and that I could
possibly love and be loved again.

—*JENNIFER WEST*
GREENVILLE, MISSOURI
💔12Y 💔1Y

• • • • • • • •

WHAT MUSIC HELPED ME THROUGH the hard times?
Believe it or not, it was bubblegum pop music: 'N
Sync, Backstreet Boys. I was working out three
hours a day, trying to regain the figure I had
when I was a teenager, and the teenage music
really helped.

—*ANONYMOUS*
KENT, WASHINGTON
💔8Y 💔5Y

• • • • • • • •

I LISTENED TO TRACY CHAPMAN'S first album over
and over again. I don't know what it has to do
with divorce, but it made me feel good.

—*ELIZABETH*
SALISBURY, NORTH CAROLINA
💔1Y 💔 💔13Y

• • • • • • • •

A GOOD GIRL-POWER MOVIE IS *Ever After*, with
Drew Barrymore.

—*ALISON*
SAN DIEGO, CALIFORNIA

Why Can't We Be Friends? Maintaining a Relationship with Your Ex

or some, it's simple: After divorcing their partners they will never communicate with them again. But for others—those with kids, those who still want to be friends—the divorce is the start of an entirely new relationship with their former spouse. And you thought marriage was hard! Read on for advice on how to get along with a person you recently referred to in quite unflattering terms.

WE ARE STILL FRIENDS. Not go-out-and-have-fun friends; there's still a lot of pain for both of us. But good friends. I still love her, even if I'm not in love with her and we can't be together.

—PETER STEUR
BRISBANE, AUSTRALIA
6Y 4Y 2Y

E-MAIL IS WONDERFUL!

—DANA
ANNISTON, ALABAMA
6Y 1Y

HEAD LINES
Best Advice and Top Tips

- Remaining amicable with your ex helps the divorce process heal faster.
- If your marriage and divorce ended badly, there is no real reason to remain friends.
- Maintaining a relationship with your ex is fine, as long as he or she doesn't mistreat or disrespect you.
- Having a friendly relationship with your ex and having a friendly relationship with his or her new partner do not necessarily go together.
- Approaching your relationship with your ex as a business relationship can help you put your feelings aside in order to get along—just as you would with a coworker you didn't like.

I FOUND A BOX OF my ex-husband's Christmas ornaments that he'd had since he was a child. I could've thrown them out and he probably wouldn't have even known, but I gave them back to him. There's no reason to be nasty. It just makes things easier if you're nice.

> —C.E.
> BEACON FALLS, CONNECTICUT
> 4Y

Bill who?

—SAMANTHA
LOS ANGELES,
CALIFORNIA
2Y 4Y

HE SAID IF I EVER WANTED TO give him my dog, he would take him. So when I moved to New York I gave him the dog. And it was fine—we are friends. I wouldn't pick up the phone and say, "Wanna meet for margaritas?" But it's over and in the past. Unless it's a threatening situation to you, why waste the energy being full of spite and hate and being nasty?

> —ANONYMOUS
> ATLANTA, GEORGIA
> 3Y 8Y

IT AIN'T OVER TILL IT'S OVER

After we separated, we said we weren't dating anyone else, but we both were. I went to our home one weekend to get some stuff—he was out of town—and I found a girl in his bed. I had told him I was coming over that weekend. I saw the girl and said, "Who are you?" She was like, "I'm your husband's friend." I said, "Why are you in my house?" She said, "I'm sorry, I'm his girlfriend, and I needed to do some laundry." I was like, "Great, that's fabulous." So I called him up. He was in Florida visiting some friends. I said, "Hello, ass-hole, I told you I was coming over this weekend. I was pretty sure you were seeing someone, but I didn't need to see this. And I didn't need to see her in my bed, the bed I was going to take to my house, the bed that, by the way, you are going to buy me new mattresses for now." He was horrified. He said, "She is not supposed to be there."

I think most people would have screamed and yelled. But I just tried my best to keep my cool. It wasn't about her. It was about the fact that my husband and I didn't get along and it came to that moment.

—SALLY
ETOWAH, TENNESSEE
💔4Y 💔2Y

EVEN AFTER THE DIVORCE IS FINAL, your role as co-parents will continue for years. I remember thinking to myself, "I know what you're thinking," as my ex-husband would walk toward my house. I was ready for battle, and he hadn't even opened his mouth. I would find myself suddenly and unreasonably angry. In time I learned to compartmentalize things. I would remind myself that I was talking to my child's father, not my ex-husband. I locked the former marriage relationship away in my brain so we could focus on our daughter.

—*MARIA ISBELL*
AUSTIN, TEXAS
💔 💔6Y

· · · · · · · · ·

IF YOUR EX IS WILLING to be a reasonable person, by all means try to return the favor. I hope for both my exes what I hope for myself—better luck and happiness. Take the lead in this if need be. If you raise the bar, the other person may even surprise you. Pretend to be the noble person you would like to be. Play the role.

—*HANK*
SAN JOSE, COSTA RICA
💔7Y 💔 💔6Y 💔 💔4Y

· · · · · · · · ·

DIVORCE DATA

First marriages that end in divorce last about an average of eight years.

TO THIS DAY, my ex-wife still wants me back. About a month and a half ago, we were in the child-support office and she kept telling me that I should leave my current wife and buy a house with her because "God doesn't want you to be married two times, just once." I believe there's only one way to handle this: You have to be blunt and honest. Tell her you're happy with your current life as it is, and then ignore everything else she says.

—*LENNARD HAYNES SR.*
HOUSTON, TEXAS
💔1Y 💔12Y 💔

REMAIN AT LEAST SUPERFICIALLY amicable with
your ex. My ex-wife remarried within a few
months of our divorce, and she and her husband
were concerned that I would be lonely at
Christmas, so they invited me to spend it with
them. I didn't go, but I could have.

—KEN D.
ATLANTA, GEORGIA
💔19Y 💔 💔20Y

. . . .

'Even if you miss your ex, don't
have anything to do with him
or her for a long time afterward,
if at all possible. It'll be better
in the long run. 🙰🙰

—M.T.
CHICAGO, ILLINOIS

. . . .

IF YOUR SPOUSE IS NOT HANDLING the divorce
right, draw boundaries from the very beginning.
For the first six months, I took all the abuse and
all his anger and tried to pacify my husband
instead of saying, "It is your job to fix your life." I
was always trying to help him and put him in a
better spot. But he would call me at all hours and
say ugly things. I needed to identify it for what it
was: verbal abuse. I should have told him, "I am
doing something that I believe in, and it doesn't
exactly match your plan. Call me later when you
want to discuss the issues."

—M.D.
CANYON LAKE, TEXAS
💔12Y 💔16Y

WHAT'S IN A NAME?

GET RID OF HIS LAST NAME RIGHT AWAY. It should be the second thing you rid yourself of, right after you get rid of him.

> —*SHARI BERG*
> *ELLERSLIE, MARYLAND*
> 💔2Y 💔 💔1Y

. . . .

CHANGING YOUR NAME gets a little trickier if you have school-age kids. If your kids are young enough to not know the difference, then change your surname and your kids' surnames back to your maiden name. But if your kids are in school and have been known by your husband's last name, you have to let them keep the name. If you want to change your name back at that point, it's OK. But leave your kids' names alone.

> —*ANDREA WEIGAND*
> *WOODWORTH, OHIO*
> 💔15Y 💔5Y

. . . .

MY WIFE CHANGED HER NAME BACK, and that's the way I wanted it. She let the kids keep my name, which I also thought was the right thing to do. I guess you could say that dealing with the names after the divorce was one of the very few things we agreed on.

> —*CARL COOKE*
> *CUMBERLAND, MARYLAND*
> 💔8Y 💔21Y

IF YOU HAVE CHILDREN, consider their ages and their feelings. The name-change decision was not hard for me as my kids are 13 and 14. They seemed to have a firm grasp of the situation, so I did discuss it with them before making my decision to return to my maiden name. I think if my kids were younger, I would have kept my married name to minimize the confusion at school and other places.

—*TRACY*
FREDERICK, MARYLAND
15Y 1Y

• • • • • • • •

I TOOK IT AS A BIG SLAP IN THE FACE when my wife changed her name back after the divorce. You can't erase the fact that we were married just by changing your name. She should have kept it. Besides, my last name is way better than hers. Her maiden name is Sporka. What the hell kind of name is that?

—*WALT BULLOCK*
BARRELVILLE, MARYLAND
17Y 10Y

IT JUST MIGHT NOT BE POSSIBLE to maintain a relationship with your ex-spouse. Right now, my ex-husband and I are in a period of no contact, although I had tried to maintain a cordial relationship. I've had to accept the reality that you can't force another person to keep in contact with you.

—*LAURA VINCENT*
SAN RAFAEL, CALIFORNIA
💔*20Y* 💔*PENDING*

• • • • • • • •

"I keep in contact with my ex-husband because I am entertained by watching his insane business ventures launch and fail, and think, 'Thank goodness that isn't my money anymore.'"

—*SARAH*
SEATTLE, WASHINGTON
💔*5Y* 💔*4Y*

• • • • • • • •

IT HAS TAKEN US A LONG TIME to develop a relationship. We've been able to put aside our resentments and be co-parents first. Whenever we have a question about how we should proceed on something that comes up, we say, "What's in the best interest of the kids?" And that's what we do. But I wouldn't say we're friends.

—*J.S.*
WYNDMOOR, PENNSYLVANIA
💔*20Y* 💔*1Y*

I STILL HAVE A RELATIONSHIP with my ex-husband. Our boys live with him, and right now we wouldn't have it any other way. He's a wonderful father, and I feel very lucky he has taken that responsibility very seriously. They adore him, and that helps me live via daily phone calls and e-mails to them. And when I get to see them, I see a reflection of him in them. We talk on a daily basis about our children's lives and how to help or complement them. Together we support the good and bad days for our children. And sometimes, my ex listens when a new "friend" in my life doesn't work out as I had hoped, and he is very supportive without being critical or judgmental about my decisions. I feel lucky.

—ANNA
PONTE VEDRA BEACH, FLORIDA
💔10Y 💔3Y

· · · · · · · · ·

MY EX AND I HAVE a business relationship. This was actually decent advice from a counselor—to treat the continuing relationship like someone you have to be nice to because you work with them even if you don't like them at all.

—BARRY
CHICAGO, ILLINOIS

· · · · · · · · ·

I HAVE NO RELATIONSHIP with my ex as he left me for his current girlfriend. He and I were supposed to remain friends and separate everything nicely; however, he cleaned out our house when I was at work. After that, I wanted no relationship at all. Don't get me wrong, I talk to him from time to time, and it is very amicable. But I don't go out of my way.

—JENNIFER
PHILADELPHIA, PENNSYLVANIA
💔5Y 💔1Y

We weren't friends in the marriage, so I really didn't expect to be friends afterwards.

—FRANCINE
MARSDEN
VACAVILLE,
CALIFORNIA
💔14Y 💔1Y

My mom has always called my dad when something around the house broke, even after their divorce. My suggestion, however, is that you do not call the ex when the plumbing bursts or something electrical zaps. Ask friends, husbands of friends, brothers-in-law, whomever, for suggestions for a trustworthy handyman or woman or contractor. Handle it yourself. Not only does it cut that tie, but it is also very empowering to be able to take care of things. That even includes car trouble. Make your own list of plumbers, electricians, roofers, and car mechanics. Build your own networks. Or learn to do it yourself!

—*Dana*
Anniston, Alabama
💔6Y 💔 💔1Y

A HAPPY ENDING

The first couple of years after our divorce, we were not nice to each other. But the wounds healed, and we got over it. We still love each other, but we can't live together. We reconnected a couple of years after our divorce. We were both single. We would call each other, and do things together. We eventually became friends. Not too long ago, my boss took everyone on a trip to Eureka Springs, Arkansas. I didn't have anyone to go with me. I knew my ex-husband loved Eureka Springs, so I asked him to go. We had a lot of fun.

—*Kim*
Chicago, Illinois
💔17Y 💔10Y

IT'S BEEN **14** YEARS NOW since our marriage ended, and I have gotten along well with him for most of the time since the divorce became final. Within a few years of the divorce he married his girlfriend, and she has made a choice to make no effort to get along with me or our children. He has been relatively easy to get along with, but the time when he and I were close friends is long over. Our interactions are always pleasant, yet distant.

—*MARGARET*
   BOULDER, COLORADO
   13Y 14Y

DIVORCE DATA

Recent estimates suggest that 50 to 70 percent of married men and women have been unfaithful.

· · · · · · · ·

IF MY EX-WIFE AND I are not seeing other people, she and I share holidays and vacations. Of course, nobody understands this, and prospective partners have usually scoffed at any notion that there was not still a romantic relationship between us. But there is not—just the love and respect born out of a shared responsibility to our child.

—*KYLE*
   FAIRFIELD, CONNECTICUT
   13Y 7Y

· · · · · · · ·

WE WERE YOUNG AND HAD KIDS, so we had to communicate. I had a lot of anger and bitterness, but I finally realized that she'd been an ally when I needed one. It's been fine since. In fact, I've had Christmas with her and our grown daughters twice in recent years. When people talk bitterly about their exes, I know they haven't processed the experience. They're blaming the other person instead of taking reponsibility for their own actions. When I owned up to all my stuff, it was a huge relief. I wasn't a victim anymore: I could move on. I think it's called growing up.

—*J.C.*
   ATLANTA, GEORGIA
   7Y 15Y

Never bad-
mouth each
other. Don't
ever be
demeaning:
keep it cordial.
We still talk
with each
other twice
a year.

—*Elizabeth*
Salisbury,
North Carolina
❤1Y ❤ ❤13Y

MY EX AND I ARE QUASI-FRIENDS after 15 years of
acrimony. Now we can speak about our daughters without a fight and really have nothing more
to discuss beyond that. He's been remarried
twice, and I don't hate him, which is surprising
given that he was my nemesis for so long. We
have nothing left to fight over, our daughters are
grown, and I am removed from his life as he is
from mine. I never thought I'd stop hating him,
but today I am absolutely indifferent to him.

—*Angela S.*
Arlington, Virginia
❤7Y ❤15Y

• • • • • • • • •

I WAS THINKING RECENTLY about how so many
major events of our relationship have a concert
to accompany them: the "I can't sleep with him
again because he brought another woman to this"
Hank III show, and the "Ok, it's really over" Pixies
show, and the most recent, "Oh, man, it's good to
see you again" Elvis impersonator show.

—*Shannon*
Seattle, Washington
❤2Y ❤1Y

• • • • • • • • •

IF THERE IS A DEATH in your ex's family after the
divorce, make sure you talk to your ex about
whether or not you should go to the funeral.
Don't just show up, even if you feel it's the right
thing to do. It could cause discomfort not just
for your ex but for members of the family that
are already suffering because of the death. Talk
it over with your ex ahead of time. If he feels
you should go, then go.

—*Ann Marie Bush*
Poland, Ohio
❤17Y ❤22Y

The loss of the friendship was probably the most traumatic outcome of the separation initially. Nowadays, we speak often and communicate via e-mail, but we have no social contact to speak of. I detest the woman he lives with. Strangely, all of his oldest friends also avoid being around this woman, so I'm not alone in my feelings.

—*Saralyn*
Chicago, Illinois
💔28y 💔10y

• • • • • • • •

Maintain as cordial relations as possible with your ex. This not only makes the divorce less stressful, but it makes life afterwards easier if you have children and must deal with your ex-spouse on an ongoing basis.

—*G.N.*
Ft. Smith, Arkansas
💔1y 💔 💔3y

• • • • • • • •

If the marriage and divorce are ugly, face it: You will never be friends. It may not be healthy for you to remain friends. Because my ex and I have a 15-year-old child, we must try to get along. But I certainly don't have to be best buds with him.

—*Anonymous*
Edmonds, Washington
💔16y 💔1y

• • • • • • • •

My former spouse is not in my life because he mistreats me. I have two girls, and I don't want to teach them that it is OK to be mistreated by a man. When he begins to treat me with dignity and respect, then I will make a choice to have him in my life. Until he does, he's completely out.

—*Leslie*
Tacoma, Washington
💔7y 💔1y

DIVORCE DATA

Two-thirds of divorces in the United States are initiated by women.

THE CRAZIEST THING I DID after my divorce was chase my ex-husband down in my car. I almost ran into his car and he drove into the police station. That's when I realized I was acting crazy. I was a fraction away from hitting him, but then I came to my senses.

—*ANONYMOUS*
CHICAGO, ILLINOIS
10Y 8Y 5Y

• • • • • • • •

I MAINTAIN A CORDIAL RELATIONSHIP with my ex-husband, but won't let him intimidate me (if I can manage it). I want the children—16 and 20 at the time of the divorce—to be relaxed about their relationship with both of us and never feel like they have to take sides. I think that's the best thing I did. If I pressed for child support, it would have become about money, not the kids. Even though they're older, they still needed support, and still need to feel reassured.

—*ANONYMOUS*
JEFFERSON TOWNSHIP, NEW JERSEY
25Y 2Y

10

Moving On: Dating and Finding Love Again

C ould it be true? After walking away from the wasteland that was your last relationship, you're actually thinking about dating again? And perhaps even finding someone to settle down with? Well, of course you are. You're human, and everyone wants to be loved and to love in return. Here's what some people had to say about taking those precarious steps into vulnerability.

I STARTED DATING AFTER SIX MONTHS. I didn't really feel it was time, but I was pushed into it by my brother, his wife and some friends: They felt it was time.

—B.E.A.
BLAN, OHIO
❤️7Y 💔8Y

REMEMBER THAT DRESS HE HATED? GET IT OUT AND WEAR IT!

—ANONYMOUS
WALNUT CREEK,
CALIFORNIA

DATING AFTER A DIVORCE is like going on the first date you've ever gone on in your life, but worse. You have all the excitement and anxiety, but you also know all the worst that the opposite sex has to offer. The best thing you can do is go somewhere that you always wanted to go with your ex but never did. Don't go somewhere that will remind you in any way of your ex. Get a clean start. It's even better if your date has never been there. Then you can both experience it for the first time.

—*TERRY HARRINGTON*
  CUMBERLAND, MARYLAND
  7Y 10Y

• • • • • • • •

USE THE DATE AS AN EXPERIMENT to see if you can be a better person. Before your first date after your divorce, sit back and analyze what you could have done better. Try to pinpoint your weaknesses as a partner. Then, go out on the date and try to work on those aspects of your personality. This is the perfect opportunity to try to get a fresh start and be a better partner with someone of the opposite sex.

—*BRENT ALEXANDER*
  MIDLAND, MARYLAND
  5Y 7Y

• • • • • • • •

I ALWAYS THINK ABOUT THAT SCENE in *Sleepless in Seattle* when Tom Hanks is going out on his first date after his wife dies. The best thing to keep in mind is that the other person is probably just as nervous as you are. Even if they have been dating more recently than you, they are still going out with you for the first time, so that will give them some jitters. Just try to relax and enjoy yourself.

—*ELANOR NICK*
  HOMEWOOD, MARYLAND
  13Y 4Y

HEAD LINES
Best Advice and Top Tips

- The first person you date after your divorce is not likely to be the next love of your life.

- Getting back into the dating scene can help boost your self-esteem.

- If you have children, don't bring your dates home to spend the night—at least not too soon.

- When looking for potential dates, steer clear of someone with the same personality and qualities as your ex.

- Don't rush to get married again until you have had some time on your own.

ONE OF THE BEST THINGS about dating after being divorced is getting a second chance to spot all the mistakes I should have picked up on the first time. For example, my husband's drinking was a problem in my marriage. Now, if I meet a guy who goes out a couple of nights a week and only has a good time when he's drinking, I don't want to be around him.

—*SAMANTHA*
LOS ANGELES, CALIFORNIA
❤2Y 💔4Y

• • • • • • • •

I FIND MYSELF HAPPIER than I've been in years. My kids are doing well, my job is going great, and I'm in love with someone new. If you'd have asked me six months ago if this was possible, I'd have thought it was crazy to even think it could happen.

—*L.Q.*
HAMPTON ROADS, VIRGINIA
❤14Y 💔2M

CHARLES AND CAMILLA notwithstanding, marriage brings nothing to me personally. It's an archaic rite I would never again subject myself to, no matter how much I loved the guy. If I love someone, that's enough. I don't need it sanctioned by a marriage.

> —*ANGELA SCHAFFNER*
> *ARLINGTON, VIRGINIA*
> 7Y 15Y

• • • • • • • •

I HAD A FLING WITH SOMEONE immediately. All I wanted to do was go out there and make out with many people. Probably looking back, it was to make sure I was OK. Then I met a guy through work who was going through a divorce, and we dated for two years.

> —*ANONYMOUS*
> *ATLANTA, GEORGIA*
> 3Y 8Y

• • • • • • • •

WHEN GOING THROUGH A DIVORCE, don't do what I did. My wife cheated on me, and I kicked her out. To try to get back at her, I went on a rampage, sleeping with a lot of women and having anonymous relationships. It's not healthy. You risk getting diseases, and it's not good for your mind.

> —*CURTIS M.*
> *ANN ARBOR, MICHIGAN*
> 3Y 4M

• • • • • • • •

ONE THING A BAD MARRIAGE will teach you once the pain goes away is that you've pretty much seen the worst. It actually made me *less* fearful of finding love again, because I was able to choose better men and discard the ones that were bad.

> —*L.A.*
> *CHICAGO ILLINOIS*
> 2Y 6Y

THE WORST THING TO HEAR #3

"How could you *not* be married?" What they're really saying is, "There's something wrong with you."

—*ANONYMOUS*
ATLANTA, GEORGIA
3Y 8Y

YOU ALWAYS HEAR THAT you find love when you're not looking, and that's how it happened for me. I was newly divorced and out with a friend when I met a guy at a happy hour at a local bar. We've now been married for eight years and have a beautiful daughter. He's a much better partner for me than my ex-husband and I feel very blessed.

—*ROBIN VELLIS*
CLARKS SUMMIT, PENNSYLVANIA
🖤*1Y* 🖤 🖤*8Y*

. . . .

" If you're going to start dating again, don't date the same type of person you married. And don't rush. Start with a friendship. "

—*P.R.*
AUSTIN, TEXAS
🖤*10Y* 🖤*28Y*

. . . .

AFTER I SEPARATED FROM MY WIFE, I immediately went to a professional introduction/dating service that focused on who I was and sought to introduce me to my ideal mate. They worked hard to set me up with likely candidates, and this gave me hope that I would find someone else with a different set of attributes than my ex. Even though I missed my ex, the novelty of being with somebody new gradually dissolved the pain and complexities involved with the ex. I started to see a new world of possibilities that eventually made me question what I ever was doing with the ex in the first place.

—*CHRIS*
SAN DIEGO, CALIFORNIA

IT'S GOING TO HAPPEN

After my divorce, I had come to a place where I decided I was just happy by myself, with my friends and my family, and I didn't need a man. I was at my friends' house getting some sun one day. They had two daughters about my daughter's age, in their twenties. This one particular day, the girls said they were going dancing that night, and we were going with them. We said, "We're old people; we aren't going." But they insisted. We got all dolled up and went dancing at a place called Michael's Cow Palace. We were having fun and dancing, and the girls said, "Look at that man over there, you have to go talk to him." I did, and we had fun!

He called a week later. He was probably the first person I'd ever met whom I could just sit down and talk to about anything. It was very new and very refreshing. People who are divorced, especially the young ones, think they're never going to find someone. But you've got to know it's going to happen.

—B.P.
KNOXVILLE, TENNESSEE
💔25Y 💔 💔1Y

I WAS VERY PROTECTIVE of myself and my daughter after I broke up with my ex-husband. No man was allowed to sleep in my house if he had a romantic interest in me. I did very few introductions to my daughter because I did not want her to get attached if I was not sure about someone. No man was allowed to think for me when I had the ability to think for myself, and I demanded respect. The way I coped was by using my mental strength and by focusing on my lifelong goals.

—*PATRICIA YOUNG*
HERNDON, VIRGINIA
💔2Y 💔22Y

• • • • • • • •

I PROBABLY STARTED DATING too soon—about three months after my divorce. My self-esteem was in the gutter. I decided to see if men were still interested in me, and they were. Was it too soon? Yes, but it did help boost my self-esteem, and I don't regret it.

—*L.Q.*
HAMPTON ROADS, VIRGINIA
💔14Y 💔2M

• • • • • • • •

NEWLY DIVORCED PEOPLE shouldn't try to go out and find someone new right away. If you push it, you're going to find the wrong person. If you just live life and put yourself in activities that are good for you (gardening or bicycling, for instance), you will eventually run into someone who shares similar interests. That's how I met my second wife. My daughter found out about a babysitting gig. The woman looking for a sitter was interested in hiring my daughter, but first she wanted to meet her parents: that's how we met.

—*THOMAS M.W. "MIKE" DOWNS*
FAYETTEVILLE, NEW YORK
💔18Y 💔 💔1Y

Because your self-esteem is at an all-time low, you tend to attract good-for-nothing men. Don't get married just to find someone to help you.

—*GEORGENE*
CRYSTAL BEACH, FLORIDA
💔7Y 💔 💔13Y
💔 💔3Y

It took years to reestablish my self-confidence and not feel like a wounded animal. At the beginning, I went out with several men and was desperate to be loved again and married. Now I couldn't care less. My divorce lasted so long and was so debilitating that I doubt that I will ever marry again.

—*Angela Schaffner*
Arlington, Virginia
💔7y 💔15y

• • • • • • • •

❝I figure, what's the worst that can happen to me if I don't find a man who makes me feel happy? I can wind up an old cat lady. But hey, I love cats.❞

—*Shannon*
Detroit, Michigan

• • • • • • • •

I started dating about eight months after my divorce, and I thought I was ready, but it was at least two years before I was able to have a whole relationship. There's a lot of emotional baggage you carry, even when you don't realize it. I'd been advised that 99 percent of second marriages fail because they happen on the rebound. I tried to pay attention to that and not be in a hurry, but I still made a bad second marriage and my ex-wife did, too.

—*M.E.W.*
Gladstone, Oregon
💔30y 💔 💔3y 💔 💔7y

I DIDN'T AVOID DATING, but I didn't bring men home either. We lived in a small neighborhood, and my son was in junior high and my daughter was not far behind him. I didn't want their friends saying, "Your mom had a strange car parked in the driveway overnight." Divorce is hard enough on kids without them having to deal with that.

—*M.D.*
CANYON LAKE, TEXAS
♡12Y 💔16Y

• • • • • • • •

THE QUICKEST WAY OUT of the pain of someone is in the arms of another. There is no such thing as rebound—the need to be with someone is always there.

—*CHRIS*
SAN DIEGO, CALIFORNIA

• • • • • • • •

FOR A WHILE, I had to lick my wounds. Then, almost three months later, I agreed to meet a male friend and his friend for cocktails. This was a great, casual way to ease back into the dating scene. It takes a lot of pressure and anxiety off you. Plus, if you decide you're not up to it after all, you can always duck out without leaving anybody alone.

—*E.C.*
NEW YORK, NEW YORK
♡2M 💔2Y

• • • • • • • •

I'D GET MARRIED AGAIN someday when I'm ready. Sharing yourself with someone in that way is a beautiful thing. The commitment is beautiful, too. But it will take time before I'm ready for a commitment on that level again.

—*RAVEN*
TACOMA, WASHINGTON
♡2Y 💔2Y

DIVORCE DATA

Divorced men are more likely to remarry than divorced women.

I discovered that the best way to find another mate is to quit looking.

—*J.S.*
  HOUSTON, TEXAS
  20Y 3Y

BE UP FRONT ABOUT THE FACT that you are divorced because you don't want it to appear later that you were keeping that from your date. But for God's sake, don't talk about your ex. Nobody wants to hear that. If she insists on asking about it, gently steer the conversation in a different direction. Every time the woman I was dating asked about my ex, I'd start talking about the Washington Redskins just to divert her.

—*JERRY ROSE*
  CUMBERLAND, MARYLAND
  13Y 12Y

• • • • • • • •

I'VE CHOSEN TO REMAIN completely celibate, for a variety of reasons, since the divorce. I don't plan to get married again, I am not looking for or interested in a physical relationship, and I expect this to be the case for the foreseeable future. Actually, I highly recommend celibacy during the divorce process, to eliminate a significant cause of conflict which can lead to vindictiveness. Being celibate diffused any issues with the ex thinking there was another woman and being upset or angry about that.

—*ALLEN R. PYLE*
  HILLSDALE, MICHIGAN
  9Y 8M

• • • • • • • •

I WAS DIVORCED FOR 30 YEARS. I think that people go from one relationship to another because they are insecure. I've never been like that. I've always been very independent. I've gone through a lot of bad relationships, made a lot of bad choices, but I never married them! My theory is that mistakes are there for us to learn from. From every mistake there's a lesson to be learned.

—*P.C.*
  DARLINGTON, MARYLAND
  5Y

THE GRASS IS NOT GOING TO BE GREENER on the other side unless you take a look at your part in the divorce. What behaviors could be changed to ensure a healthier relationship in the future? The better you know yourself and what you really need in a partner, the better your chances will be for success. I think the best thing I did was to not have a sexual relationship with my present husband until we built a friendship and really got to know each other. Slow and steady wins the race.

—*ELIZABETH*
CHATTANOOGA, TENNESSEE
💔1Y 💔 💔6Y

JUST ONE LOOK

A fter my second failed marriage, I decided that I would never get married again. A couple of years later, my son was diagnosed with cancer, and I put all of my energy into getting him healthy again. Six months later, a girlfriend invited me to a dance for singles that our church sponsored. I resisted going with her, but finally did. As I looked at the dance floor, I wondered what I was even doing there. I certainly wasn't looking for a guy, and nobody there looked like someone I even wanted to know. I turned around to leave and ran into the biggest guy I had ever seen (6' 4", 350 pounds). I said, "Oh, do you want to dance?" We have been dancing ever since. My son has been in remission for 14 years.

—*DIANE EVANS*
RENTON, WASHINGTON
💔8Y 💔 💔6Y 💔 💔13Y

WHEN I MET THE WOMAN who would be my second wife, we had both been divorced. To clear the air, one night we had "sad story night" when we talked about our previous marriages and painful divorces. That night really helped us to learn where the other person was coming from and set the groundwork for our new relationship.

—*M.R.*
HELLERTOWN, PENNSYLVANIA
2Y 1.5Y

• • • • • • • •

IT'S BEEN MORE THAN FOUR YEARS since my last divorce, and I am now living with a woman that I adore. We have both decided that maybe for us, being on our better behavior is not such a bad thing at all. Between the two of us, we have had five marriages in total. I can honestly say that I have never been happier, so I really hope it can last and last. If not, at least I have had this time with her.

—*HANK*
SAN JOSE, COSTA RICA
7Y 6Y 4Y

WHEN YOU START DATING AGAIN, date consciously. Differentiate between the qualities you like in a date, and the qualities you realized you need for day-to-day happiness in a marriage. For example, I married a man who was fun, outgoing, exciting, and ambitious—all things I liked. But I wasn't happy because he didn't make a good husband. We could have fun together, but I didn't respect and admire him, and he didn't treat me like I was special. I learned that marital satisfaction counts more on character than on personality.

—*LIZ*
NEW YORK, NEW YORK
💔1Y 💔 💔1Y

LOOKING FOR MR. THROWAWAY

When I did get involved with someone new, I learned a truth that I always share with friends in similar situations: The first relationship after a divorce is a throwaway. I call the guy I got involved with my throwaway man. It sounds awful, but the first relationship after a long-term marriage typically is a rebound situation—good for having fun, but in my case not someone I would ever consider having a long-term relationship with. The more I got to know him, the more I could see that he fit certain criteria that I had deprived myself of—he satisfied my wild side, and it was good to get that out of my system.

When I met my second husband, I wasn't looking. I was happy with my life the way it was. My second marriage has lasted for 20 years.

—*ANONYMOUS*
WAKEFIELD, NEW HAMPSHIRE
💔8Y 💔 💔20Y

SINCE I WAS ALREADY EMOTIONALLY detached by the time we actually got divorced, I began dating right away. It took several months to get my freedom out of my system and settle down.

—*J.S.*
HOUSTON, TEXAS
💔20Y 💔3Y

• • • • • • • •

Try not to date the same person you just divorced. I don't mean the exact same person; just the type.

—*ALEXIS*
KNOXVILLE, TENNESSEE
💔5Y 💔2Y

AFTER A FEW EXCITING yet unsustainable relationships following the marriage, I made a decision not to remarry. I have liked living life independently and have really blossomed during this phase of my life. I am certainly open to dating and/or friendships with men. And yet I do so well on my own, I might just remain single for the foreseeable future!

—*MARGARET*
BOULDER, COLORADO
💔13Y 💔14Y

• • • • • • • •

DON'T SHOW A POTENTIAL DATE your Web site if you post pictures of ex-girlfriends and conquests.

—*M.H.*
SAN ANTONIO, TEXAS
💔10Y 💔4Y

• • • • • • • •

IF YOU'VE BEEN MARRIED and therefore out of the dating loop for a while, a good way to find out what's going on and the good places to hang out is the Internet. You can just Google your hometown, and you will find several good sites about the hot spots in town—where they are, who the clientele is, what people wear, what the hours are; everything you need to get started finding Mr. Right.

—*BERNICE ZLATOS*
YOUNGSTOWN, OHIO
💔10Y 💔21Y

DON'T START DATING; you are not yet in the right frame of mind. It's easy for women who are used to being in a relationship to get swept up by some nice gentleman providing attention. After you process your divorce, you will be in a better place to make sound judgments on picking your next partner.

—*DAWN PETCHELL*
ARLINGTON, VIRGINIA
2Y 1Y

* * * * * * * *

'Stop being embarrassed about letting someone know you are interested. Didn't you do that whole embarrassment thing in junior high and high school? Who wants to be back there?'

—*S.P.*
REDMOND, WASHINGTON
13Y 3Y

* * * * * * * *

IT'S VERY DIFFICULT to launch yourself socially as a single woman; it's easier for men. Call up your friends. Try to keep busy doing things with people you enjoy. If you get depressed and withdraw, no one can help you. If you just wait around to be invited, you might not be. It was helpful to make new friends who didn't have a relationship with my ex-husband; it was easier to move on when I found a place in a world he had no part of.

—*ANONYMOUS*
GREENWICH, CONNECTICUT
45Y 1Y

ONLINE DATING

WHEN I WAS READY TO START DATING AGAIN, I joined an online dating group called *oneandonly.com*. I met a lot of nice people there, including my second wife. It's an easy, comfortable way to meet a lot of people. I recommend meeting for the first time in a very public place, though, just in case she's an ax murderer!

> —*M.R.*
> *HELLERTOWN, PENNSYLVANIA*
> 💔2Y 💔 💔1.5Y

• • • • • • • •

I MET PEOPLE ON JDATE AND MATCH.COM and made new friends in my area that helped me to get over my ex. If you use dating as a learning process, it's helpful. But if you use it to meet someone to marry, it could be discouraging.

> —*ANONYMOUS*
> *CHICAGO, ILLINOIS*
> 💔10Y 💔 💔8Y 💔5Y

• • • • • • • •

SEVERAL YEARS AFTER MY DIVORCE, I've been meeting men through online dating services. It's been a great way to meet people. One guy I've met, though he isn't going to be my soul mate, is a terrific friend. We have a lot in common and often talk for hours at a time. What has been most wonderful, though, is to get his male perspective on life in general and divorce and dating in particular. Men think so differently than women; his opinions have been very helpful to me.

> —*L.G.K.*
> *EASTON, PENNSYLVANIA*
> 💔23Y 💔5Y

AFTER I LEFT, I had a totally silly fling with this guy in a band. He was really cynical and annoying and funny, and it kind of makes me squirm to think about it because the whole thing was so dumb in a way. But it was just what I needed. After it was over, I went into my reclusive, licking-my-wounds stage, but I needed that little confidence booster before I could start the task of getting to know myself again.

—*A.P.*
CHAPEL HILL, NORTH CAROLINA
3Y 2Y

· · · · · · · ·

SEX HAS BEEN VERY LIBERATING since my separation. My ex-wife was very critical of everything I did sexually. I waited a year before I slept with another woman; when I did, it was a wonderful feeling to find women who appreciated and enjoyed sex with me. In fact, after 48 years, I'm now learning new things in the bedroom that I didn't know before!

—*ANONYMOUS*
WESTON, MASSACHUSETTS
12Y PENDING

· · · · · · · ·

IT'S DIFFICULT TO MEET PEOPLE to date when you're a divorced guy. Women can sense the kind of desperate, needy screw-up that most divorced men are. And you've been off the market for years, so your skills are rusty. But you just have to put your face out there, and you'll meet somebody through friends. I met a woman and dated her for four years. It was a fantastic relationship, and it was amazing to be in a healthy, honest, committed relationship. It was totally validating. It taught me that I wasn't totally screwed up.

—*EVAN*
ATLANTA, GEORGIA
1Y 5Y

CHUBBY HUBBIES

One study found that men who remarry start packing on the pounds and cutting back on exercise, compared with men who remained unmarried.

DATING IS A LOT MORE FUN NOW that I'm older. But if you think that older men are more mature and more honest than younger men, think again. Once you realize that, you can have a lot more fun.

—S.P.
REDMOND, WASHINGTON
💔13Y 💔3Y

• • • • • • • •

THE HARDEST PART WAS realizing that I would have to get back in the dating scene again. Dating was never easy for me. But after our divorce, I knew that eventually I would start dating again. That made me even more angry at my ex-husband. How did I do it? I just developed a plan of how I was going to meet men, bought one new outfit, and went out.

—M.R.
VALLEJO, CALIFORNIA
💔 💔35Y

• • • • • • • •

WOMEN, JUST BECAUSE you are divorced doesn't mean you are dead! You will have sexual urges! Fulfill them in creative ways; you don't need a guy. You won't be ready for that for a while. Do not be ashamed of your body or of sex. It is a natural and beautiful thing.

—ANONYMOUS
EDMONDS, WASHINGTON
💔16Y 💔1Y

• • • • • • • •

DON'T GET MARRIED AGAIN until you're pretty sure of who you are as a person. Once you've established yourself clearly, you can then find someone who complements you. While you're in the process of changing or doing a lot of growing, you don't know who you are, much less who you should be with.

—M.C.L.
CHAPEL HILL, NORTH CAROLINA
💔 💔 💍

The Road Ahead: Healing From Your Divorce

Your divorce has been a defining moment for you: The key is to learn from it, let go of it, move on, and grow. In this chapter, we offer stories from people who used the experience of their divorce to make their lives better: When they looked back, they smiled at what they had accomplished.

I SPENT SO MUCH TIME BEING BITTER. What a waste! I was finally free, able to start again, and this jerk was still ruining my day? Let go, be thankful, move on.

—AMY
DURHAM, NORTH CAROLINA
7Y 3Y

THERE ARE DAYS THAT ARE TOUGH. AND THERE ARE DAYS WHEN EVERY-THING IS RIGHT WITH THE WORLD.

—ANONYMOUS
EDMONDS,
WASHINGTON
16Y 1Y

HEADLINES
Best Advice and Top Tips

- Taking time to do things for yourself—gardening, meditating, taking classes—is an important survival strategy.

- Let yourself be angry; it's an essential part of the healing process. You may find that freeing yourself from a bad marriage leaves you feeling happier than you ever thought possible.

- Learn something new: Involve yourself in a hobby, craft, or activity that you have never done before.

- Embrace your newfound freedom: It is the best thing to come out of your divorce.

The biggest change in myself is a feeling of adventure and independence. There is a whole new life to live.

—*G.D.*
CHICAGO, ILLINOIS
💔17Y 💔1Y

I HAVE BEEN HAPPIER SINCE THE DIVORCE than I ever was before. I never got to know myself in marriage, and what I have discovered is that I am a really interesting person! I don't think I ever would have known so much about myself if I had not been divorced. Like, who would have known how much I like to travel, or how much I like margaritas?

—*G.H.*
CHAPEL HILL, NORTH CAROLINA
💔23Y 💔20Y

• • • • • • • •

LET YOURSELF GET ANGRY! When I got divorced, I was sad and depressed, but if you don't access your anger it causes even more depression. A friend of mine took me out to a driving range one day and said, "Hit those balls!" It helped me to get some of my anger out. Find what works for you; you could hit a punching bag at the gym or pound chicken while you cook.

—*SHARON NAYLOR*
MADISON, NEW JERSEY
💔6Y 💔6Y

I ALWAYS THINK OF all the miserable things that my ex-husband did to me, and I try to recapture those moments in my head. I have a journal in which I wrote down all of his negative aspects, as well as all the horrendous things he did to me, and all the countless lies he told me. When I get to feeling melancholic, all I have to do is open it up, and there is my instant reminder of how truly better off I am.

> —SHANNON
> DETROIT, MICHIGAN

* * * * * * * *

IT TAKES SOME TIME, but you will not be truly healed until you can stop beating up both yourself and your spouse for what happened. Once you do that, you will feel like the weight of the world has been lifted off you.

> —COLIN MCDOUGLE
> CANFIELD, OHIO
> 14Y 20Y

* * * * * * * *

IT PROBABLY TOOK ME TWO YEARS before I was over my divorce. Early on you get to the point where you might stab your ex through the heart if you have a dagger nearby. But forgiveness is crucial to healing.

> —BEA BETTERS
> POLAND, OHIO
> 4Y 6Y

* * * * * * * *

I RECOVERED FROM THE TRAUMA of the divorce by going back to school to study one of the fields my ex-husband excelled in: I did better in it than he ever has. There is nothing better than beating out your ex.

> —SARALYN
> CHICAGO, ILLINOIS
> 28Y 10Y

IT'S YOUR LIFE

Now that the divorce is final, you may be wondering what in the world to do with yourself. For many, this time of divorce is the dawn of self-discovery and personal renewal.

I TOOK COLLEGE COURSES, got a new job, began a spiritual and religious investigation, and made new friends who were not part of the old social circle.

> —JAMIE TEAL
> NATICK, MASSACHUSETTS
> 3Y 3Y

• • • • • • • •

AS SOON AS I GOT DIVORCED I took up conga drumming. It was the only time I felt happy. It was something I always wanted to do, so after the divorce I had time and went once a week on Sundays. I didn't think of anything else when I was drumming.

> —ANONYMOUS
> CHICAGO, ILLINOIS
> 10Y 8Y 5Y

• • • • • • • •

I TOOK A CLASS IN STAND-UP COMEDY. Five minutes of bashing my ex-wife in a room full of laughing strangers was better than any therapy I ever received.

> —G.D.
> CHICAGO, ILLINOIS
> 17Y 1Y

• • • • • • • •

I DISCOVERED THAT I LOVE CYCLING. I have joined bike clubs and taken many long bike rides through forests, over mountains, and even on volcanoes! It is a great activity that I love, but I had not realized it until after my divorce.

> —DOUG
> WAIKOLOA, HAWAII
> 5Y

ONE THING THAT KEEPS ME GOING IS my love for reggae, dancing, and writing. Get a young haircut and buy books by the author Sark. Don't dwell on the bad things that you can't change: Embrace the new, the unknown. Get excited: I am. I am apartment-hunting tomorrow, looking for a place that will belong to me. Bought by me, for me.

—ANONYMOUS
EDMONDS, WASHINGTON
16Y 1Y

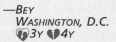

I'D GIVEN UP MY AMBITIONS of performing stand-up comedy because the hours were such a strain on our relationship. Now, with the apartment empty, it was the last place I wanted to be at night. I started going to open mics every night. The comedy was cathartic: I could bitch about my marriage and win approval for my ranting. The freedom was wondrous.

—BEY
WASHINGTON, D.C.
3Y 4Y

AMONG THE MANY MEANINGFUL and fulfilling hobbies I acquired during my divorce, I am proud to say that I am now an expert quilter.

—FRANCINE MARSDEN
VACAVILLE, CALIFORNIA
14Y 1Y

I LOST WEIGHT, ran races, and hired a personal trainer. I also moved to the city from the country so I could be involved in more activities.

—ANONYMOUS
KENT, WASHINGTON
8Y 5Y

I ENROLLED IN CLASSES. I traveled. Maybe most important, I took some time for just me and reevaluated my life.

—*MARY WEBB*
WHEELING, WEST VIRGINIA
❤21Y 💔21Y

• • • • • • • • •

I'M ON THE SKI PATROL, and I rock-climb—two things that I never tried while I was married. I also enjoy dating. I've met so many great people who would never have entered my life while I was involved with my wife.

—*ANONYMOUS*
WESTON, MASSACHUSETTS
❤12Y 💔PENDING

• • • • • • • • •

DO THINGS YOU ALWAYS WANTED TO DO, like take a painting or poetry class, or write a book. Get in touch with childhood friends if possible. Take a cross-country trip. Go to Europe. Dress too young (get it out of your system). Join a local political group. Go camping. Eat by candlelight. If you don't have a furry pet, get one.

—*TERRI B.*
GOLDENS BRIDGE, NEW YORK
❤21Y 💔1Y

AFTER A DIVORCE, in order to move on, you have to take responsibility for your poor decisions. I made the decision to marry—a bad decision—and I needed to get over that. First, you have to acknowledge to yourself that you made a bad choice. Our bad marriage is a result of my decision, and I learned from it.

—*ANONYMOUS*
CHICAGO, ILLINOIS
🖤*10Y* 💔 🖤*8Y* 💔*5Y*

• • • • • • • •

WHAT HELPED ME SURVIVE my divorce was working in my garden. One of my friends noticed that I was calmest when I was in the garden, so when I would get anxious and crazy about the divorce, she would say, "Get into the garden!" I didn't realize just how much it helped me until she pointed it out. Now, whenever I'm facing something difficult or stressful, the garden is my retreat. I can release some of my feelings in the physical work of digging and raking, and I can focus my attention outside myself.

—*B.A.*
PORTLAND, OREGON
🖤*7Y* 💔*28Y*

• • • • • • • •

SPEND SOME TIME ALONE MEDITATING, or exercising, or with close friends, reviewing who you are, where the ground is, and what's absolutely essential in your life. Find spiritual help that works for you. Above all, don't forget that—God or no God—life is essentially absurd. Keep laughing at its marvelous ludicrousness; even point out goofy things to others if that's safe and appropriate. The cliché is, "Keep your sense of humor."

—*ARCH*
LONDONDERRY, VERMONT
🖤*18Y* 💔*1Y*

NEW HORIZONS #1

Having a hard time meeting new women? Head to Latvia, where 54 percent of the population is female and only 46 percent is male.

Being divorced has opened my eyes to lots of things. One of the biggest lessons I've learned is that people make mistakes. It's taught me a lot about forgiveness— of myself *and* others.

—*ANTHONY MANUEL*
KINDER, LOUISIANA
14Y *4Y*

IF THERE'S SOMETHING that you felt the marriage was preventing you from doing, just do it. For example, I was held back from going to school because I had to support my wife. Before I got married, my income was enough to support me, the bachelor, but afterwards she wasn't pulling her weight. The divorce allowed me to go back to school and complete some programs, which put me in a position for a better salary.

—*SHAWN W. HARWARD*
SAN ANTONIO, TEXAS
2Y *5Y*

. . . .

TAKE ADVANTAGE OF ANY POSITIVE opportunities the divorce presents. When I got divorced, I realized that I could live anywhere in the world I wanted to. It was overwhelming and liberating to have so many choices. After a lot of thought, I narrowed it down to Santa Fe, New Mexico, and the San Francisco area. I felt at peace in both places. I paid attention to that feeling. I chose the San Francisco area, and I've been very happy out here.

—*LAURA VINCENT*
SAN RAFAEL, CALIFORNIA
20Y *PENDING*

. . . .

DON'T SECOND-GUESS YOURSELF about getting divorced. A few years ago, when I was talking with my second son, I casually mentioned that maybe I shouldn't have divorced his father. "Are you kidding me?" my son asked. "Look at the difference you have made in people's lives as a parenting instructor since then. You never would have done that if you'd stayed married." I was so grateful that he had reminded me.

—*SUSIE WALTON*
SAN DIEGO, CALIFORNIA
19Y *14Y*

FOR ME, HEALING WAS AND IS A PROCESS of deepening my faith in God, and also being sure to share my pain with other people who are compassionate. The separation from my children stirred up very deep fears and hurts from my separation from my own father. I think there is such a thing as "father hunger," the need for a father figure. Healing is a process of rediscovering our own unconscious longings as grown-up children.

—*WILLIAM DUCHON*
MILFORD, CONNECTICUT
7Y 1Y

· · · · · · · ·

I make a conscious effort to live life better: to not be in bad relationships, to do things I've always wanted to do but put off. I'm happy right now.

—*EVAN*
ATLANTA, GEORGIA
1Y 5Y

· · · · · · · ·

SINCE MY DIVORCE, I got into Columbia and London business schools and received my MBAs from them. I took my experience and my education and started my own business. What I've accomplished I'm sure I wouldn't have done if I were still married to him. I just wouldn't have thought outside the box. We were living in the suburbs, and talking about getting pregnant, and we had two dogs.

—*ANONYMOUS*
ATLANTA, GEORGIA
3Y 8Y

THE BENEFITS OF THE HIGH ROAD

I had many good reasons to be angry with my husband and divorce him. But the rest of his family took his side. I was so hurt and angry that I cut off almost all communications. Because of my daughter, there continued to be contact, but it was strained at best.

A year later, I started to get my life back together and move on. At the same time, a door opened for healing my relationships with my (now affectionately called) "out-laws." I went to them and said, "You and I are family and always will be, especially because of my daughter. I love you all and want us to be part of each others' lives again." They didn't quite know what to say, but they had seen how I forgave their son.

Their reply came a week later when my sister out-law came to me. She said I was the closest thing she ever had to a sister, and she wanted me to be in her bridal party the following spring. And so it was: I was part of the bridal shower, the bachelorette party, and the wedding day. My daughter was the flower girl, and we were in all of the pictures. I brought my new boyfriend (now husband), and it felt really good to be there, part of the family again. We even sat at the table with my ex and his wife.

—SUSAN
SOUTH SALEM, NEW YORK

EVEN IF YOU THINK YOUR DIVORCE was not your fault and you did nothing wrong, there is still a lot to learn from the experience. I knew my divorce was not my fault, but my therapist said a few words that put everything into perspective for me: "You chose him." Meaning, I may not have done anything wrong, but I was making poor judgments when it came to relationships. I am confident that I will have a much more satisfying marriage and family life next time around because of what I learned about myself and relationships in therapy.

—*LIZ*
NEW YORK, NEW YORK
🐛*1Y* 💔 🐛*1Y*

· · · · · · · ·

NEW HORIZONS #2

Having a hard time meeting new men? Move to the United Arab Emirates, where there are two men to every woman.

THERE IS DEFINITELY A PROCESS that has to happen. Pain and hurt from whatever made the marriage fail will cause a lot of tears. Then comes anger! Then all of a sudden, a sense of peace comes and you realize how good it feels to be happy, whether you are by yourself or in a new relationship. If there are children, you come to realize that you have now created a healthy environment for them by getting out of a bad marriage. Finally, you'll get to the point when you see him during visitation weekends and you smile at him and say to yourself, "I'm *so* glad that's someone else's problem now!"

—*FRANCES*
POWAY, CALIFORNIA

· · · · · · · ·

I AM LESS AFRAID OF TAKING CHANCES. I don't need the security (emotionally or financially) that I used to need. I am happier on my own than I ever thought I would be.

—*ALEXIS*
KNOXVILLE, TENNESSEE
🐛*5Y* 🐛*2Y*

Dump the baggage, get the monkey off your back, move on, and have a happy, productive life!

—*LESLIE YOUNG*
TACOMA,
WASHINGTON
💔7Y 💔1Y

SINCE MY DIVORCE, I'm not as critical of myself for not making things perfect. And I'm more accepting of others' flaws. I do things to make myself smile at no risk to anyone but myself. And I've learned to include my friends in my life decisions. I don't feel I have to be quite so independent.

—*ANNA*
PONTE VEDRA BEACH, FLORIDA
💔10Y 💔3Y

. . . .

MY BIGGEST CHANGE IS that I protect myself and my assets like Scrooge did his money. I am so afraid of being left high and dry. So, maybe I am paranoid now? But I'd rather be safe than sorry.

—*KIMBER VELARDE*
SAN DIEGO, CALIFORNIA
💔3Y 💔 💔1Y

. . . .

I'M LESS LIKELY TO COMPROMISE on the things that genuinely matter. My lifestyle is much more down to earth (Bohemian?), and I'm clothed more casually than during my married life. It feels good.

—*JOHN ANTHONY*
WASHINGTON, D.C.
💔6Y 💔11Y

. . . .

SADNESS WAS THE OVERWHELMING feeling that I experienced during the divorce and still feel today even though I'm happily remarried. I am very sad that our marriage failed. Sad for our children. Sad for our grandchildren. And sad for us as grandparents unable to share the joy of our grandchildren together. Fifteen years later, I still feel some sadness. But I've learned to live with it. Life goes on!

—*INGELA KOPONEN*
SWEDEN
💔20Y 💔 💔14Y

I READ THE BOOK *What Color Is Your Parachute,* which has exercises that make you dig deep inside to match up your skills with a job, and further tells you how to go about finding the job that suits your personality. I found other skills aside from being a stay-at-home mom that translated into job skills. I think that book, coupled with taking classes, is what shaped me and my career. I was 36 years old when I had my first sales job, and I eventually started my own business. That was a very gratifying experience.

—*DEE DEE MELMET*
SONOMA, CALIFORNIA
🖤10Y 💔 🖤3Y 💔21Y

• • • • • • • •

LEARN HOW TO FORGIVE. Let it go. I have met people who are bitterly hostile 10 and 15 years after their divorces. I've been through it, so I know that your relationship with your ex-spouse is one that can turn you into a screaming idiot overnight.

—*MARIA ISBELL*
AUSTIN, TEXAS
🖤 💔6Y

• • • • • • • •

MY HUSBAND KILLED MY SELF-ESTEEM and then he told me how much he missed the happy, confident woman that he had married. Since he left, I have found the self-esteem he stole. When you are being lied to and cheated on, you want to believe the lies and deny the cheating—especially when the other person tells you it is all in your mind. You question your own sanity. Well, he is gone and I am quite sane, thank you. I accomplished much more as a single woman than I ever had during the marriage, so I get excited when I think about what the future holds.

—*ANONYMOUS*
MARIETTA, GEORGIA
🖤*PENDING*

SPLIT-UP STAT

In November of 2004, a 48-year-old woman became the first person in Chilean history to file for divorce. Prior to that, there was no divorce law in Chile, a heavily Roman Catholic country.

WHEN I WAS MARRIED, my husband controlled the finances, our expenses, bank accounts, etc. Now I know exactly where I stand and don't need anyone to help me pay my bills or give me advice or tell me what I can and can't do. I'm finally self-sufficient. I see now that I am not meant to be married.

— *ANGELA SCHAFFNER*
ARLINGTON, VIRGINIA
7Y 15Y

• • • • • • • •

CONSIDER JOINING A DIVORCE RECOVERY GROUP or taking a Beginning Experience Weekend. This is a program that helps people resolve their grief from separation, divorce, or even death. Beginning Experience challenged me to rediscover myself, and I found some great talents that I had long forgotten.

— *IRENE VARLEY*
SARASOTA, FLORIDA
22Y 17Y

• • • • • • • •

I SIMPLY DECIDED I was not going to let my divorce ruin my life. I thought to myself, "One of two things could happen here: I could let this turn me into a sad, lonely person, or I could choose to start a new, even better life." I made a major effort to reach out to my friends and family. I contacted old friends and visited out-of-town friends over weekends. I started a group that I called The Adventurers' Club and planned activities for all of my female friends. We went to a local winery's grape-picking party and to a corn maze. It really helped me to move on with my life, surrounded and supported by my friends.

— *JENNIFER REICH*
HELLERTOWN, PENNSYLVANIA
7Y   2Y

I WENT TO A DIVORCE RECOVERY GROUP at my church. It was helpful to have the support of other people going through the same thing that I was, even though the situations all varied. I made some good friends through that process. I am currently looking for another support group, as I think that women who are victims of domestic violence need some special care and assistance. I do not fear repeating my pattern, but I want to heal from it so that I don't take any old behaviors into my parenting or my future relationships.

—*LESLIE*
TACOMA, WASHINGTON
♡7Y ♡1Y

* * * * * * * *

TWO MONTHS INTO MY DIVORCE, I am planning a trip with a divorced friend. I've never flown in a plane before, and I'm flying. I just wanted to do something I would never have done before. I want to live. I want to be crazy for a while. I just want to enjoy life.

—*JENNIFER WEST*
GREENVILLE, MISSOURI
♡12Y ♡1Y

DIVORCE FINAL, KIDS PENDING

In 2005, the governor of Washington state signed a bill allowing pregnant women to divorce their husbands. Prior to that, and if interpreted strictly, Washington's child-support law prevented a pregnant woman from divorcing her husband until the baby was born and paternity could be determined.

I REMEMBER TALKING TO a good friend and co-worker about my divorce. He had gone through a divorce himself. He said, "One day you'll wake up in the morning, and you'll realize that this whole divorce thing isn't really all that bad. You'll wake up refreshed, thinking that it's all behind you and it's time for you to move on." That was six years ago. Today, I realize that my friend was right: The pain of divorce seems to dissipate over time. I finally realize that I have my whole life ahead of me, and it is time for me to move on.

—*JERRY*
OAKLAND, CALIFORNIA

• • • • • • • • •

WHEN YOUR MARRIAGE ENDS, you shouldn't put blame on the other person. If you can't be honest with yourself, there will be deception in every part of your life. I went through the annulment process in order to have the option to marry again in the church. In the questionnaire I filled out, no blame could be put on my spouse. It took me over a year to be able to answer those questions, but it was helpful for me to look inside and see my responsibility in the breakup. After doing this, it was like a weight was lifted off my back.

—*RAY PEREZ*
HOUSTON, TEXAS
💔4Y 💔10Y

On the Other Hand: Best and Worst Things About Divorce

'D*ivorce is great." "Divorce is horrible." "Divorce taught me things." "Divorce ruined my life." We asked people the best and worst things about divorce. Starting with the worst and ascending to the best (mirroring how we hope your life evolves), we offer their answers here.*

THE WORST IS THE LONELINESS. I just think people are meant to be with another person of the opposite sex. And when you get used to having someone there it's a big adjustment when they're gone. I would come home from work for months after the divorce still expecting to find her there.

—FRANK CAPISO
BOARDMAN, OHIO
💔10Y 💔10Y

ARE YOU KIDDING? OBVIOUSLY IT'S THE LACK OF SEX.

—BARNIE VERONA
BOARDMAN, OHIO
💔 💔13Y

The hardest part about getting a divorce was the thought of failing at something. I was already used to sleeping alone at night, due to his raunchy night-time rendezvous.

—SHANNON
DETROIT, MICHIGAN

THE IDEA OF HAVING TO START dating again. Talk about a scary proposition: I was married for 16 years and hadn't been on a date for about 19 years. I didn't even know where to begin. But if you want to date, you have to be aggressive and get over your fears. I will someday.

—LEROY BROWN
BRADDOCK, PENNSYLVANIA
16Y 2Y 1Y

· · · · · · · ·

THE WORST PART OF MY DIVORCE is definitely the alimony. Maintaining her livelihood suddenly becomes a full-time job, and your own livelihood is shot to shit.

—ROBERT HARRIS
LOS ANGELES, CALIFORNIA
15Y 5Y

· · · · · · · ·

THE WORST THING ABOUT A DIVORCE is feeling like a failure because the marriage didn't work out. It's difficult to give up on a dream, a place you've considered home, and an intact family for your children. It can feel quite devastating. You have to have courage. It's easy to see why people stay in dysfunctional relationships.

—LINDA
FALMOUTH, MAINE
30Y 1Y

· · · · · · · ·

THE HARDEST PART HAS BEEN getting over my ex. I still love him very much and wish we could be together. We're trying to be friends now, but I want more than that. But as painful as it is, I don't want to stop trying, because I want so badly for him to be part of my life. I have dreams that he'll change his mind and come back to me.

—SARAH
WASHINGTON, D.C.
5Y 1Y

THE HARDEST PART IS the physical moving out, the absence of the other person and their belongings. The emptiness of the closets was the hardest part for me.

—*ANONYMOUS*
CHICAGO, ILLINOIS
💔10Y 💔 💔8Y 💔5Y

• • • • • • • •

Now there's nobody to say, 'You shouldn't eat ice cream before bed'; to look at me funny when I do my spa-like treatments; to bother me while I curl up on the couch with my favorite romance. ""

—*ANONYMOUS*
EDMONDS, WASHINGTON
💔16Y 💔1Y

• • • • • • • •

THE HARDEST PART ABOUT GETTING DIVORCED? The feeling that I had failed. I am a lawyer who has started a successful law practice, so I was accustomed to succeeding at what I really worked hard for. But when my marriage failed, I was devastated. When my divorce became final, I took time away from practicing law and just comforted myself. I took a long vacation and tried new activities like scuba diving. I loved it. I quickly forgot about my ex-wife and any thoughts of failure!

—*DOUG*
WAIKOLOA, HAWAII
💔 💔5Y

THE WORST THING TO HEAR #4

Her name, or any mention of your ex-wife. It just got to be so painful to hear anybody talking about her in any way. Even when friends of mine said bad things about her, it hurt.

—CLAYTON MCLEOD
LOWELLVILLE, OHIO
8Y 4Y

THE WORST THING ABOUT BEING DIVORCED is the healing period, the immediate time after. When I first got divorced I felt empty; I felt like I lost out on an investment: Marriage is an investment, and I lost a lot of time and emotion on mine.

—BONNIE LAMB
CHICAGO, ILLINOIS
15Y 13Y

. . . .

THE WORST WAS SEEING MY SON feel so stressed about his parents splitting up. We both decided to be totally committed to making his life as stable and happy as possible. He is our number one priorty.

—MONIKA JENKINS
JEFFERSON, MARYLAND
10Y 5Y

. . . .

THE HARDEST PART IS no longer being a part of a couple, and having that status and safety. You're on your own, lost and alone, and basically you feel dead inside.

—ANGELA SCHAFFNER
ARLINGTON, VIRGINIA
7Y 15Y

. . . .

THE HARDEST PART IS making the decision to leave: I sat and watched my wedding video I don't know how many times. I come from a divorced home and never wanted that to be me. Another hard stage is leaving your married life behind. I lived in a wonderful, beautiful house and had to sell it and go back to the single-girl life living in a condo. I remember standing in a 700-square-foot condo and thinking, "I can't believe this is my new life."

—DAWN PETCHELL
ARLINGTON, VIRGINIA
2Y 1Y

THE HARDEST PART WAS applying for public aid on my 26th birthday (and being turned down because I owned my car), and hiding the news from my parents. I didn't want them to be upset, and I didn't want a handout.

—*L.M.*
CHICAGO, ILLINOIS

• • • • • • • •

THE HARDEST PART IS accepting the fact that I am now a divorce statistic. I thought it happened to other people and that working hard to have a dual income and be a high-profile couple was what we both wanted. I didn't think he would say he felt neglected.

—*ANNA*
PONTE VEDRA BEACH, FLORIDA
💔*10Y* 💔*3Y*

• • • • • • • •

THERE IS NOTHING MORE DIFFICULT than leaving your children when you leave your marriage. It hurts me every day that I can't raise my two daughters full-time. This has been the saddest part of my divorce and my life.

—*ANONYMOUS*
WESTON, MASSACHUSETTS
💔*12Y* 💔*PENDING*

• • • • • • • •

THE HARDEST PART WAS LEAVING the house where I'd lived with my husband and our dog. I drove away in a moving van. I was crying, and the dog was looking at me through the window like he did every day when I left for work. This time I wasn't leaving for work.

—*LISA*
NEW YORK, NEW YORK
💔*1Y* 💔*3Y*

One of the best and worst things about divorce is that you will learn who your friends are.

—*ALEXIS*
KNOXVILLE, TENNESSEE
💔*5Y* 💔*2Y*

DEALING WITH MY BITTER EX-WIFE: For years I tried to understand why she did the things she did. At some point I just gave up looking for understanding and decided that I can only look forward.

> —G.D.
> CHICAGO, ILLINOIS
> 💔17Y 💔1Y

• • • • • • • •

THE WORST THING TO HEAR #5

How he had moved on and about all the young girls he was dating. I knew most of it wasn't even true, but it still bothered me.

—MAUREEN BYRD
CALLA, OHIO
💔3Y 💔 💔1Y

THE WORST THING IS NOT HAVING my tall husband around to reach things on the high shelves in the kitchen. Come to think of it, that's not only the worst thing about being divorced, but it's the only negative I can think of. And I can get a step stool that won't cheat on me.

> —A.G.
> HUBBARD, OHIO
> 💔11Y 💔2Y

• • • • • • • •

FEELING LIKE A FAILURE: I was really young, and we shouldn't have gotten married in the first place, but I still felt like a failure.

> —ELIZABETH
> SALISBURY, NORTH CAROLINA
> 💔1Y 💔 💔13Y

• • • • • • • •

ADMITTING I WAS A VICTIM OF ABUSE and realizing our three children were in the middle of all of the horror.

> —ANONYMOUS
> INDIANAPOLIS, INDIANA
> 💔10Y 💔8Y

• • • • • • • •

NOW THAT I AM REMARRIED and soon to graduate from college, I have proved to my ex and mostly to myself that I can get through rough times and still survive.

> —WANDA M.
> BALTIMORE, MARYLAND
> 💔11Y 💔 💔2Y

ONE AND THE SAME

For me, the best and worst things about being divorced were the same: I was alone and I had to learn to be an adult and to take full responsibility for my child. I also had to come to terms with the realization that I wouldn't have successful relationships until I could learn to be alone with myself. That was a big revelation. At first I yearned for the companionship and security of a relationship, but I didn't want to make the mistake of falling back into old patterns. The best thing about my divorce was that I would never have done the wonderful things I *have* done in the 20-plus years since. All the traveling I've done, the fun experiences I've had, and the people I've met—I wouldn't give those up for anything! They've enriched my life tremendously.

—Anonymous
Des Moines, Iowa

THE BEST THING ABOUT BEING DIVORCED has been the freedom to learn who I am. I didn't do that before I got married and then I found out afterwards that I'd skipped a vital step in life.

—*LISA*
NEW YORK, NEW YORK
💔1Y 💔3Y

• • • • • • • •

PROBABLY THE BEST PART of my life with my son (my hero) is everything. From the heartaches of returning him to his mom, to the laughter over whipped cream on his nose, to the intense times with his therapist, and the moments we shared when I was the assistant coach of his hockey team. Single parents should just love their children unconditionally, and realize this is a first for the parent and child. It is a growing pain and learning curve for both, and they will learn and grow together.

—*ROBERT R. FITZSIMMONS*
ISLANDIA, NEW YORK
💔3Y 💔21Y

• • • • • • • •

✔

Best part:
No more
floral patterns
on the bed
sheets.

—*E.P.*
CRANBERRY
TOWNSHIP,
PENNSYLVANIA
💔7Y 💔18Y

THE BEST THING ABOUT DIVORCE is feeling like I regained control of my life. For years, I had known that things weren't right but I felt paralyzed to do anything about it. Once I was on my own, I could make decisions to improve my life.

—*KRISTI*
AUSTIN, TEXAS
💔8Y 💔7Y

• • • • • • • •

I GUESS THE BEST THING IS that it made me realize what I do want in a marriage and a husband. I realized that I wanted to be with someone considerate, and more giving of himself, and someone who gets along with many people.

—*ELIZABETH*
SALISBURY, NORTH CAROLINA
💔1Y 💔 💔13Y

I HAVE GROWN UP. I am learning to do things on my own. All because I am not depending on anyone else to take care of me.

> —*H.O.*
> *EVERETT, WASHINGTON*
> 💔2Y 💔1Y 💔1Y

• • • • • • • •

 The best thing about my divorce was that I got to raise my children as I chose, without much interference. It also tested all my strengths, because as a single parent you have to do it all. 🙶

> —*PEG*
> *DENVER, COLORADO*
> 💔7Y 💔25Y

• • • • • • • •

THERE WERE A LOT OF GOOD THINGS about my divorce: It drew me much closer to God, since my ex had no respect for my religion. (I am a Christian Scientist.) I finished my dissertation; it taught me to survive on my own, including learning how to cook on a wood stove when the power goes out. If I hadn't gotten a divorce, maybe I wouldn't have grown in my faith; maybe I never would have finished the dissertation. To me this is like the story of Joseph in the Bible. Despite Joseph being tossed in a hole and left to die by his brothers, God had a larger purpose in mind for him.

> —*M.S.*
> *SEATTLE, WASHINGTON*
> 💔5Y 💔13Y

IS THERE A BEST PART OF DIVORCE? I think it's in the beginning of the actual separation, when the person who has been belittling you and beating you down is no longer in your day-to-day life.

—L.K.
KING WILLIAM, VIRGINIA
2Y 1Y

THE MOST WELCOME PART for me was when the final decree came down after a year of being separated. We were both relieved that we could get on with our own lives and go about raising our son—together, but separately.

—KYLE
FAIRFIELD, CONNECTICUT
13Y 7Y

THE BEST PART OF THE DIVORCE for me is the quality time I have with my daughter. I have her at least three nights a week, more than most fathers. My daughter and I have a great relationship, and she will always be my best memory from a marriage gone bad.

—G.D.
CHICAGO, ILLINOIS
17Y 1Y

THE FREEDOM. There is something very exhilarating about knowing that your life is all yours again. It's sort of like a death, but at the same time it's sort of like a rebirth, too. It's like you have a chance to do whatever you want all over again. That's a feeling that you slowly and quietly lose when you are in a serious relationship. I found that I didn't even know it was gone until I got it back.

—STACEY YURICK
LEETONIA, OHIO
1Y 1Y

THE BEST THING IS THAT I don't have to worry anymore about what he may or may not be doing. Now that we're divorced, I don't care what he's doing.

> —*D.P.*
> *IRWIN, PENNSYLVANIA*
> 17Y 4Y

• • • • • • •

I FEEL BETTER ABOUT MYSELF being away from this person. I like myself and the energy of my home. It feels like home again, and a safe place. This is very important, especially when raising children.

> —*LESLIE*
> *TACOMA, WASHINGTON*
> 7Y 1Y

• • • • • • •

THE BEST PART OF MY DIVORCE WAS knowing that I can have a peaceful home once again—no more arguing!

> —*SHANNON*
> *LAS VEGAS, NEVADA*
> 2Y 12Y

• • • • • • •

THE BEST PART OF OUR SEPARATION has been the opportunity (albeit forced) for me to think about who I really am and to invest in me. After five months, I still don't have any answers, but it's liberating to take charge of my own path in life.

> —*SARAH*
> *WASHINGTON, D.C.*
> 5Y 1Y

• • • • • • • •

THE BEST PART OF THE DIVORCE WAS knowing I could and would now have control of my life back and the children would not only be safe but have a calm place to live and be happy.

> —*ANONYMOUS*
> *INDIANAPOLIS, INDIANA*
> 10Y 8Y

CIAO, BABY (TAKE THREE)

In May of 2005, an Iranian woman requested a divorce from her husband on the grounds that he had not washed for more than a year.

THE BEST PARTS: freedom, liberty, breathing space. I just didn't appreciate how much of my passion and personality I'd suppressed only to avoid friction and conflict. Gaining back the independence to go, do, be as I pleased was awesome. The end of regular reminders about what was incomplete, missing, inadequate, yet to be done, etc., was absolutely emancipating.

—*JOHN ANTHONY*
WASHINGTON, D.C.
💔6Y 💔11Y

. . . .

" One of the best things is knowing that if I put something down, it's going to be in the same exact spot when I get home. "

—*C.E.*
BEACON FALLS, CONNECTICUT
💔4Y 💔

. . . .

THE BEST PART WAS KNOWING that I would never have to share a meal or a bed or a bank account with this man ever again. I would never have to wonder if he was home when I got there and what kind of a mood he would be in. I could spend *my* hard-earned money the way I pleased without asking his permission. But most of all, the best part is that my boys would be all right under a new roof. *My* new roof.

—*EVE C.*
NEEDHAM, MASSACHUSETTS
💔5Y 💔7Y

THE BEST PART OF MY DIVORCE WAS swallowing my pride and taking one of three jobs paying $8 an hour—not getting public aid, not taking any handouts, but surviving without getting the child support he was supposed to pay, but didn't. I made it.

—*L.M.*
CHICAGO, ILLINOIS

. . . .

I NEVER LOST SIGHT OF MYSELF and what I have always believed in. If you want good things to happen, they will.

—*ANNA*
PONTE VEDRA BEACH, FLORIDA
💔10Y 💔3Y

. . . .

MONEY WAS ALWAYS AN ISSUE with my ex; I was never making enough. Interestingly, I made a few million in real estate in the five years since my divorce. Funny how things change so quickly.

—*ADAM*
CHICAGO, ILLINOIS

. . . .

MY DIVORCE MADE ME REALIZE that the life I fantasized about, and never thought I'd have while I was still married, is attainable. What you want might not have been possible in your last relationship. But if you imagine your desires, you can and will manifest them in your next relationship. Sure, you'll have other problems to tackle with a new person, but you'll be grateful that you listened to your authentic self and didn't deny yourself what's truly important to you.

—*ANONYMOUS*
SAN FRANCISCO, CALIFORNIA
💔5Y 💔1Y

It was a relief to not have to listen to any more of his poorly conceived lies, and to not hear the sound of his mother's bloodcurdling voice, or his annoying friends, and to not have to act amused during sex.

—*ANONYMOUS*
DETROIT, MICHIGAN

It's just knowing I did the absolute best thing for myself. I love my new life.

—*HAWLEY HUSSEY*
BROOKLYN,
NEW YORK
💔 💔*2Y*

I BEAT DEPRESSION! I was diagnosed with clinical depression during the time our marriage was falling apart. I was on a downhill track to becoming suicidal. The best part of my divorce is that I have overcome the dreadful disease and I am no longer on medication, and I'm much more confident and happy—finally!

—*BECKIE*
SEATTLE, WASHINGTON
💔*4Y* 💔*2Y*

. . . .

I WORKED SO HARD trying to keep my marriage together, that I don't have regrets—I don't feel like I just ran out on a marriage. The best thing about divorcing is that I regained my integrity, and left a relationship that was becoming abusive.

—*QUISQUEYA DE LA ROSA*
MARGATE, FLORIDA
💔*2Y* 💔*1Y*

. . . .

THE BEST THING ABOUT GETTING DIVORCED is that now I can be myself, I don't have to try to be something I'm not (which never works anyway), and now the two of us are free to pursue our lives without holding the other back.

—*WALTER MCMAHAN*
AUSTIN, TEXAS
💔*13Y* 💔*1Y*

More Wisdom: Good Stuff That Doesn't Fit Anywhere Else

T*he route through a divorce is clearly marked by the many travelers who have gone before you, as the earlier chapters have described. There's more wisdom, captured by hundreds of our respondents, that defies categorization, yet you need to hear it. Read on.*

DO WHAT IS RIGHT, not necessarily what is easy. You have got to live with yourself when the divorce is over.

—*ALEXIS*
KNOXVILLE, TENNESSEE
💔5Y 💔2Y

FORGE AHEAD AND LOOK BACK AS LITTLE AS POSSIBLE.

—*DAVID FEDER*
DES MOINES, IOWA
💔5Y 💔 💔8Y

HEAD LINES
Best Advice and Top Tips

- Be prepared for surprises: you may find happiness when you least expect it.

- Don't stay married for the sake of the children; it will only hurt them in the end.

- Try to learn from your mistakes, and take responsibility for your part in the failed marriage.

- There is no shame in getting divorced; the shame is staying in an unhappy marriage.

- Don't look back.

YOU HAVE TO TAKE RESPONSIBILITY for your own happiness. Getting divorced was both the smartest and hardest thing I ever did. But I don't regret it for a minute. That experience taught me not to let society or family pressure me into doing something with my life because other people think I should.

　　　—*JOANNE WOLFE*
　　　　NESKOWIN, OREGON
　　　　8Y 2Y

They say there are two women for every man—it took me two tries to find the right one.

—*JIM McADAM*
　PRESQUE ISLE,
　WISCONSIN
　16Y 25Y

IF YOU'RE A PARENT and you're unhappy in your marriage, please don't stay married "just for the sake of the kids." My parents did this, and it has done far more damage than good. As a result of their unhappy union, I find it next to impossible to trust relationships. I cheat on or fight with my boyfriends constantly, and I emotionally distance myself from everyone.

　　　—*ANONYMOUS*
　　　　CASTLE ROCK, COLORADO

THERE IS NO FAIRY-TALE MARRIAGE where you wake up each morning to greet the day with a smile because you have the best partner and the most loving, understanding relationship in the world. Instead, in marriage you wake every day and grit your teeth until the next day comes, because you think, "What the hell have I gotten myself into?" and, "What will it cost to get me out?"

—*S.M.*
DETROIT, MICHIGAN

. . . .

The best advice I received was: Don't take it personally. It doesn't matter if it was you or any other dude in that same position. She would have acted exactly the same.

—*BRIAN JOHNSON*
SAN DIEGO, CALIFORNIA
3Y 3Y

. . . .

WOMEN TODAY ARE LUCKY because at least they can talk about their divorce and have it known that they are divorced without being ostracized. It wasn't always that way. Back when I got divorced, people didn't talk as openly about it as they do now. It was like your own dirty little secret. Now, you don't have to hide it or be ashamed. Be thankful that at least we've come that far.

—*ROBIN LALLY*
GREENFORD, OHIO
2Y 28Y

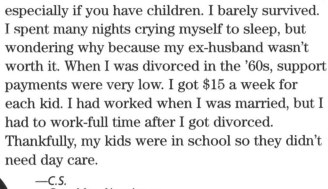

DIVORCE IS THE MOST DIFFICULT THING in the world, especially if you have children. I barely survived. I spent many nights crying myself to sleep, but wondering why because my ex-husband wasn't worth it. When I was divorced in the '60s, support payments were very low. I got $15 a week for each kid. I had worked when I was married, but I had to work-full time after I got divorced. Thankfully, my kids were in school so they didn't need day care.

—*C.S.*
CAPE MAY, NEW JERSEY
11Y

• • • • • • • •

YOUR NEXT HUSBAND is not going to be any better than your first. There is no perfect life, and none of us are entitled to have it, and none of us will achieve it. It's too bad that wisdom comes too late.

—*GEORGENE*
CRYSTAL BEACH, FLORIDA
7Y 13Y 3Y

• • • • • • • •

I NEVER DID ANY OF THE VENGEFUL, hateful things that I could've done during my divorce, and guess what? Karma did kick in. I moved to the next state over and met a wonderful guy. We married and still I was never mean or hateful to my ex or his new wife. When we all got together, I just acted like she didn't exist. I have to admit, though, that the greatest joy ever was going back to visit my old neighbors' house and hearing from her that the "other woman" said I was so lucky because I had the greatest husband! She was jealous of me.

—*ANONYMOUS*
WESTERVILLE, OHIO
7Y 11Y *AND ABOUT TO GET MARRIED FOREVER*

THE TRUTH SHALL SET YOU FREE

To be honest, I didn't think I'd ever get over my ex-wife. She was one of those one-in-a-million women who carried herself like a queen. The day she told me she cheated on me, my mind went numb. It was like seeing the end of the world, and it hurt, and it felt like I might never recover.

For our entire marriage, maybe our entire relationship, I had always second-guessed myself. I remember feeling that large parts of our relationship felt like we had just been together to not feel alone. We lacked a foundation where we could be ourselves. We were never comfortable with that. It was always painful introducing each other to friends from work because it was two different worlds. And we knew that.

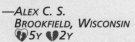

So when she finally told me the truth behind the affair and what she wanted to do, it took some thinking, but it was free-dom. For the first time in six years, I was living life honestly.

—*Alex C. S.*
Brookfield, Wisconsin
💔5y 💔2y

I WOULD NEVER HAVE GOTTEN THROUGH the process if I didn't pray and go to the mental health clinic once a week for one and a half years! Now, I am past that, but I still pray.

—*PEGGY*
SEATTLE, WASHINGTON
💔11Y 💔7Y

• • • • • • • •

" I'm not bitter; that's self-defeating. I avoid thinking of the past. I'm happy now with the peace and quiet that I chose; I'm doing what I want, when I want. I have my cat, my books, and my friends. "

—*ANONYMOUS*
💔22Y

• • • • • • • •

TO THOSE WHO CAN'T SEE THE LIGHT, I think it's important to try opening your eyes first. There was a period of four months after my ex told me it was over where nothing mattered and my heart literally ached every day. But the truth was that the more I realized I had a second chance at being the best person I can be, the more my heartache turned to the feeling of triumph that I could really live.

—*ALEX C. S.*
BROOKFIELD, WISCONSIN
💔5Y 💔2Y AND ABOUT TO GET REMARRIED FOREVER

MY EX AND I WERE simply oil and water, and no matter how much effort you apply trying to blend them, they will never truly blend. As long as water remains water and oil remains oil (in other words, as long as we stayed who we were individually), it was only a matter of time until our differences became pronounced and difficult to manage.

—*WALTER MCMAHAN*
AUSTIN, TEXAS
💔13Y 💔1Y

* * * * * * * *

WHAT WOULD I DO DIFFERENTLY? I think I'd be accountable for my part of the things that didn't work, and I'd try to learn from it. I didn't do that for a long time. I blamed him and that really didn't help. But afterwards, when I started being accountable, I saw there were a lot of things I could have changed about myself that would have made things better.

—*ANONYMOUS*
ATLANTA, GEORGIA
💔12Y 💔7Y

* * * * * * * *

ANY WAY YOU LOOK AT IT, divorce sucks for every single person involved, including the people that have to listen to you talk and cry about it for months, even years, after the fact. But surviving divorce does take time and a lot of support. You may never truly get over it, and you will definitely be a different person because of it. But as time goes by, you begin to understand and accept why it happened and, most important, that it's most likely better that it did. Hopefully your friends won't be completely sick of you by then.

—*ANONYMOUS*
SAN DIEGO, CALIFORNIA

To cope with my divorce, I got a girlfriend who is 20 years younger and bought a Corvette. It has worked out well.

—*ROY MOORE*
SPRING BRANCH, TEXAS
💔18Y 💔1Y

IT HAS BEEN MEDICALLY PROVEN that it takes more muscles to frown than it does to smile. So please wake up every day and walk out of your front door with a smile on your face. You gave yourself a fresh start with your divorce—take advantage of it. You never know who is watching you smile.

—*STACEY SAMUELS*
CHICAGO, ILLINOIS
💔2Y 💔2Y

• • • • • • • •

"**Be prepared for surprises! My divorce wasn't my idea. I finally had to give in to it. It turns out, however, that I'm much happier now than I was when I was married. Boy, I was a lucky one!**"

—*ANONYMOUS*
EAST BRUNSWICK, NEW JERSEY
💔25Y 💔6Y

• • • • • • • •

I DEPENDED ON MY OTHER INTERESTS to get through my divorce. Make sure your life doesn't revolve around your relationship. The hurt and disappointment of being rejected is lessened if you have a job and hobbies and a life outside your marriage.

—*ANONYMOUS*
DOUGLASVILLE, GEORGIA
💔18Y 💔 💔11Y 💔7Y

I BROKE A PROMISE I MADE TO MYSELF when I was younger that I would only get married once in my lifetime and I would stay with that person. Whether that is an idealistic and silly notion or not, to this day it still cuts me deeply that I could not keep my promise. Because I made a really bad choice, I'll never have the first time again. It's gone.

> —*RAVEN*
> *TACOMA, WASHINGTON*
> 💔2Y 💔2Y

. . . .

TRY TO SEE THE GOOD SIDE OF THINGS. There is nothing wrong with getting a divorce. I think trying to hang on when someone else doesn't want to anymore is one of the biggest wastes of time. If they don't want to stay, don't make them. There is a lesson to be learned in everything; try to figure it out.

> —*H.O.*
> *EVERETT, WASHINGTON*
> 2Y 💔 1Y

. . . .

THE ONLY TIME YOU EVER really feel like you've divorced your ex is when he dies. This is especially true if you have children together, because parenting issues continue to haunt you over and over again: child support; custody battles; discipline. It never goes away.

> —*TINA KUNZER-MURPHY*
> *LAS VEGAS, NEVADA*
> 14Y 💔19Y

It's not possible to fully survive divorce—it always leaves a permanent scar.

—*D.M.*
IOWA CITY, IOWA
💔20Y 💔25Y

I RECALL BREAKING DOWN and trying really hard to hide my emotions while in a bookstore looking for books dealing with this difficult subject of surviving divorce. (It's helpful that these days, many things can be ordered online!)

—*HECTOR*
ELMWOOD PARK, ILLINOIS
💔9Y 💔

• • • • • • • • •

EVEN THOUGH DIVORCE CAN BE PAINFUL, try to see the blessing in it. You were obviously not married to the most compatible person for you, or to the person with whom you can live your happiest life. Now you have a chance, and the power, to find the person that is your best fit. Some people stay unhappily married for the rest of their lives because they are too afraid to end it. Not you. You had the courage to give yourself a second chance and a new beginning. Enjoy it.

—*LIZ*
NEW YORK, NEW YORK
💔1Y 💔 💔1Y

• • • • • • • • •

VERY OFTEN WHEN A FAMILY has to watch a loved one suffer a terminal illness for an extended duration, when the loved one dies there is a sense of relief and gladness that the suffering is over, and so it is with my marriage—its death was inevitable, but my life will go on. Holding on to the past is detrimental. When you're driving, how much time is spent looking ahead, and how much time is spent looking in the rearview mirror? It's impossible to move forward the best we can while we are so busy looking behind.

—*WALTER MCMAHAN*
AUSTIN, TEXAS
💔13Y 💔1Y

I LEARNED THAT YOU ARE NOT THE SAME person at 16 as you are at 18. You are not the same at 18 as you are at 21. You're not the same at 21 as you are at 23. And you sure as hell aren't the same at 23 as you are at 30.

—BETH
ATLANTA, GEORGIA
5Y 5Y

* * * * * * * *

I guess there's this thing called 'the dance' in relationships, and I missed all the steps! It's a good learning experience for my next relationship.

—ALISON
SAN DIEGO, CALIFORNIA

* * * * * * * *

YOU HAVE TO REMEMBER that no matter how bad it is now, it's going to get better. Without my ex-wife in my life, I have found sanity, serenity, and a feeling of inner peace. Once you're not living in the daily drama, your perspective will change.

—DAVE
GREENBELT, MARYLAND
8Y 1Y

AS THE SONG GOES, "Regrets, I've had a few . . ." However, as I look back I don't think I'd change a thing. As totally incompatible as we were, we sent four very wonderful compositions of DNA down the pike toward eternity. We had four great children!

—*BILL STRAIN*
KERRVILLE, TEXAS
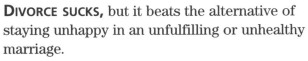*21Y   35Y*

. . . .

DIVORCE SUCKS, but it beats the alternative of staying unhappy in an unfulfilling or unhealthy marriage.

—*ANONYMOUS*
INDIANAPOLIS, INDIANA
10Y   8Y

. . . .

I HAVE NOTICED A TREMENDOUS CHANGE in myself since the divorce. I am now an outgoing, happy person who deals with any and all difficult issues in a positive, head-on manner. How I moved on after our divorce was to not continue to be a victim. I sought some therapy for the children and myself, and I went back to work after being a stay-at-home mom for 10 years. I also pursued my modeling career after being told for many of those 10 years how ugly, fat, and stupid I was. To date, all has proven to be successful for me and the children.

—*ANONYMOUS*
INDIANAPOLIS, INDIANA
10Y   8Y

DIVORCE
INFORMATION

GETTING A GRIP ON COSTS

Legal assistance doesn't come cheap, but there are some steps you can take to keep the costs from getting out of control. The most important thing to remember when consulting an attorney is that time is money.

BE ORGANIZED WHEN YOU SEE YOUR DIVORCE ATTORNEY. This is especially important for your first meeting. The more organized you are, the more efficiently you will be able to go through the particulars of your situation.

COMMUNICATE CLEARLY WITH YOUR LAWYER. It is important that your lawyer know as much as possible about you so that he or she can best represent you. Never assume your lawyer knows something if you haven't directly told him or her.

IN ADDITION TO CONSULTATION AND COURT-APPEARANCE FEES, there are a myriad of other charges you should be prepared to pay once you decide to hire an attorney. You will be responsible for all expenses related to your case, including:

Filing fees and court costs

Photocopying and faxing

Long-distance telephone
 charges

Postage and messengers

Investigators

Paralegal, secretarial, and
 staff time

Deposition and court reporter
 costs

Process servers

Travel expenses

ALWAYS LOOK CLOSELY AT YOUR BILL to ensure that you are not being charged any fees and expenses that were not agreed upon.

THE DECISION TO DIVORCE AND ITS IMPACT

*N*o *matter how right the decision to divorce might feel, deciding to actually go through with it is never easy. And the process of managing years, even decades, of shared finances, personal possessions, and memories is an emotional rollercoaster few are prepared for. Add children to the mix, and it is not a decision to be taken lightly. The impact of divorce affects all members of the family in different ways.*

FOR HUSBANDS AND WIVES: Obviously divorce often creates a great emotional upset for husbands and wives going through it. Some researchers believe it can take women an average of three and a half years to regain a sense of balance and stability in their lives. For men, that number is believed to be much shorter, in part because men tend to have more financial stability and a greater support system to lean on during the process.

While there is much truth in the old adage "time heals all wounds," for some, the trauma from a divorce is one that they are never able to overcome—particularly those whose identity is closely linked to their marriage. All individuals going through a divorce generally experience a period of self-centered behavior, and a drop in their ability to function normally. In many cases, parents are focusing on their own emotional pain and it impacts their parenting skills by making them less available to address their children's needs. Generally, these conditions are temporary, but for those who find themselves unable to recover, the impact on their behavior becomes chronic.

FOR CHILDREN: It is common for a child's first reaction to the news of Mom and Dad divorcing to be a fear of abandonment by both parents, not just the one moving out. Children often focus on the logistics of life for the parent who is leaving: where he or she will live, how he or she will be taken care of, etc. Physical reactions are also common, including trouble sleeping and, in younger children, bed-wetting.

The most important consideration parents can make is in how they decide to tell their children the news of their divorce. Dramatic statements, such as that Mom or Dad just left, can be most damaging. Conversely, assuring them that the "divorce doesn't change anything" is also ill-advised. The best approach is to be as honest with your children as possible. Explaining concretely which specific aspects of their life will change (living arrangement, school, etc.), and reassuring them that no matter what changes occur, the divorce is not their fault, will go a long way in helping children make the transition.

TAKING THE HIGH ROAD

*W**hen** you are in the throes of a divorce, emotions (and tensions) are running high. Your first instinct isn't necessarily to be on your best behavior. In the end, though, the more even-tempered you can be, the easier the whole thing will be on you. Here are some suggestions for things you should and shouldn't do if you want to make your divorce as painless as possible.*

DO

- Try to compromise with your ex, no matter how angry you are. It will put an end to the whole process more quickly.

- Remember that divorce is harder on your children than it is on you.

- Be truthful about your assets and property. If a court learns you have lied about your finances, it can void a divorce decree and you will have to start the whole process all over again—even many years later.

- Be sure to talk to your attorney and get an explanation of anything in the proceeding that doesn't make sense to you—no matter how small the question may seem.

DON'T

- Make plans to relocate until your divorce is final. It may unnecessarily delay the end of your marriage as well as the start of your new life.

- Put your children in the middle. Obey any temporary custody or visitation orders until you have your day in court.

- Be spiteful and try to hide possessions so your spouse can't ask for them—you will find yourself in court later if you are caught.

- Try to handle the process without an attorney if you have a large amount of assets and property at stake.

20 DOCUMENTS YOUR DIVORCE ATTORNEY WILL REQUEST

*O*nce you've decided to seek legal counsel for your divorce, the *best—and most economical—approach to take is to be as prepared as possible at your first meeting with your attorney. The following documents are among those you should be prepared to present to your attorney. Make photocopies of everything.*

1. Income tax returns for the past three to five years (federal, state, and local)
2. Proof of current incomes
3. Bank statements
4. Pension/retirement account statements
5. Trusts
6. Stock portfolios
7. Mortgages
8. Property tax statements
9. Credit card statements
10. Loan documents
11. Utility bills
12. Monthly budget worksheet
13. Benefits statements
14. Life insurance and health insurance policies
15. Homeowner's insurance policies
16. Automobile insurance policies
17. Property appraisals
18. List of personal property, including home furnishings, jewelry, artwork, computers, home office equipment, clothing and furs, etc., listing what was owned by each spouse prior to the marriage, and what was acquired during the marriage.
19. List of contents of safety deposit boxes
20. Wills

ISSUES TO DISCUSS WITH YOUR DIVORCE ATTORNEY

*Y*ou may not find it easy to think straight in the middle of this highly charged process, but there are many practicalities that need to be addressed when creating a divorce settlement. You don't want to make it through the whole ordeal only to find you've skipped over some crucial issue. Below is a list of topics you want to be sure to address with your attorney.

❏ Child support

❏ Child custody and visitation for the noncustodial parent

❏ Visitation for grandparents

❏ Children's college education

❏ Equity in home

❏ Home furnishings

❏ Business assets

❏ Retirement benefits (pensions, IRAs, 401(k) plans)

❏ Motor vehicles

❏ Savings accounts, stocks, bonds, and funds

❏ Spousal support

❏ Compensation for contributions made as a homemaker

❏ Health coverage

❏ Beneficiaries of life insurance policies

❏ Hidden assets

❏ Debts

❏ Nonfinancial support after the divorce is final

❏ Returning to a maiden name

❏ Legal fees

CHILD SUPPORT

*W*hile the specific laws regarding child support vary from state to state, one thing is true across the board: Both parents are expected to be responsible for the financial well-being of their child or children, regardless of whether the mother and father separated, divorced, or were never married in the first place. Unlike child custody disputes, which can be a very gray area, the amount of financial responsibility that each parent bears is based on a concrete mathematical calculation that is derived from each parent's financial statement. In addition to your yearly income tax returns (including all deductions), the following are monthly expenses you should include when preparing your financial statement for the court.

- ❏ Rent or mortgage
- ❏ Utilities
- ❏ Medical insurance
- ❏ Uninsured medical expenses for yourself and your children
- ❏ Life insurance
- ❏ Auto insurance
- ❏ Homeowner's/renter's insurance

- ❏ Car payment
- ❏ Student loan(s)
- ❏ Credit cards
- ❏ Day care/babysitting
- ❏ Groceries
- ❏ Take-out food
- ❏ Restaurants
- ❏ School lunches
- ❏ Food and clothing

POST-DIVORCE ACTIONS

You've made it over all the hurdles of getting divorced—divided your belongings, agreed on alimony and child support, and signed your name on all the dotted lines. It's all over . . . or is it? Once the paperwork is complete and you're ready to start your new life as a single person, there are still some details that need to be addressed. Below is a post-divorce checklist to get you started:

❑ Change the title and registration on your automobile and notify the insurance company of changes in vehicle ownership, the number of drivers, and your address.

❑ Be sure to take your name off any debts and loans that you are no longer responsible for.

❑ For women who change back to their maiden names: Notify the Department of Motor Vehicles, your bank, and the Social Security Administration of the change.

❑ If you move, apply for a driver's license with your new address.

❑ Notify your creditors that you have moved.

❑ Open new bank accounts and apply for credit in only your name.

❑ Take your ex's name off your lease or mortgage.

❑ Change the beneficiary on your life insurance policy.

❑ Write a new will.

SPECIAL THANKS

Thanks to our intrepid "headhunters" for going out to find so many respondents from around the country with interesting advice to share:

Jamie Allen, Chief Headhunter

Andrea Fine	Helen Bond	Nicole Lessin
Andrea Syrtash	Jade Walker	Pete Ramirez
Barton Biggs	Jennifer Blaise	Robin Lofton
Besha Rodell	Joanne Wolfe	Sara Faiwell
Christina Orlovsky	Kazz Regelman	Sara Walker
Connie Farrow	Ken McCarthy	Shannon Hurd
Elizabeth Edwardsen	Laura Roe Stevens	William Ramsey
Graciela Sholander	Lisa Jaffe Hubbell	
Heather Leonard	Natasha Lambropoulos	

Thanks, too, to our editorial advisor Anne Kostick. And thanks to our assistant, Miri Greidi, for her yeoman's work at keeping us all organized. The real credit for this book, of course, goes to all the people whose experiences and collective wisdom make up this guide. There are too many of you to thank individually, of course, but you know who you are.

CREDITS

Page 3: *The Divorce Sourcebook*, Dawn Bradley Berry, JD, McGraw-Hill, 2nd edition, October 1, 1998, p. 1.

Page 9: *The Divorce Sourcebook*, Dawn Bradley Berry, JD, 1998, p. 2.

Page 10: "World Divorce Statistics," *www.DivorceMagazine.com.*

Page 11: "World Divorce Statistics," *www.DivorceMagazine.com.*

Page 28: "The Top Ten Myths of Divorce: Discussions of the most common misinformation about divorce," by David Popenoe, National Marriage Project of Rutgers University.

Page 29: *Don't You Dare Get Married Until You Read This! The Book of Questions for Couples*, Corey Donaldson, Three Rivers Press; Rev. Update edition, May 22, 2001, p. 2.

Page 37: *The Good Divorce: Keeping your family together when your marriage comes apart*, by Constance Ahrons, Ph.D., Bloomsbury, 1994.

Page 39: "Harper's Index," *Harper's Magazine*, July 2004.

Page 45: "Children and Divorce," American Association for Marriage and Family Therapy.

Page 49: "Preventive Sessions After Divorce Protect Children into Teens," National Institutes of Health.

Page 53: "World Divorce Statistics," *www.DivorceMagazine.com.*

Page 59: "The Unexpected Legacy of Divorce: A 25-Year Landmark Study," by Dr. Judith Wallerstein.

Page 63: Divorce Online, *www.divorceonline.com.*

Page 66: "Divorce—Talking About Fears and Concerns," American Academy of Pediatrics, 2000.

Page 72: "World Divorce Statistics," *www.DivorceMagazine.com.*

Page 76: "World Divorce Statistics," *www.DivorceMagazine.com.*

Page 83: "Reforms increase Divorce rate in China," International Herald Tribune, March 3, 2005.

Page 87: *The Good Divorce: Keeping your family together when your marriage comes apart*, by Constance Ahrons, Ph.D., Bloomsbury, 1994.

Page 95: *Cooperative Divorce*, by Caryn S. Lennon, *www.DivorceNet.com*, July 2004.

Page 101: "Olin Fellow Heather Mahar Examines Prenuptial Agreements," Harvard Law School, September 2003.

Page 107: *The Divorce Sourcebook*, Dawn Bradley Berry, JD, 1998, p. 35.

Page 113: "The Top Ten Myths of Divorce: Discussions of the most common misinformation about divorce," by David Popenoe, National Marriage Project of Rutgers University.

Page 119: "A Discussion with Elizabeth Warren," *Harvard Law Today*, March 2002.

Page 123: 2004 American Psychological Association Survey.

Page 127: *The Divorce Sourcebook*, Dawn Bradley Berry, JD, 1998.

Page 131: *The Divorce Remedy: The Proven 7-Step Program for Saving Your Marriage*, Michele Weiner Davis, Simon & Schuster, September 10, 2001, p. 22.

Page 137: *www.amazon.com.*

Page 139: *www.amazon.com.*

Page 144: "Number, Timing, and Duration of Marriages and Divorces: 2001," U.S. Census Bureau, February 2005.

Page 151: *The Divorce Sourcebook*, Dawn Bradley Berry, JD, 1998, p. 37.

Page 153: *The Divorce Remedy: The Proven 7-Step Program for Saving Your Marriage*, Michele Weiner Davis, Simon & Schuster, September 10, 2001, p.39.

Page 163: "The State of Our Unions 2004: The Social Health of Marriage in America," The National Marriage Project at Rutgers University.

Page 166: "Cohabitation, Marriage, Divorce, and Remarriage in the United States," *Vital and Health Statistics*, Series 23, Number 22, Centers for Disease Control and Prevention.

Page 167: "The State of Our Unions 2004: The Social Health of Marriage in America," The National Marriage Project at Rutgers University.

Page 172: "Remarriage Turns Men Into Couch Potatoes," *Journal of Epidemiology and Community Health*, January 2005.

Page 173: "Cohabitation, Marriage, Divorce, and Remarriage in the United States," *Vital and Health Statistics*, Series 23, Number 22, Centers for Disease Control and Prevention.

Page 179: Guinness Book of World Records online.

Page 183: Guinness Book of World Records online.

Page 186: *www.msnbc.com.*

Page 187: *www.msnbc.com.*

Page 199: *www.msnbc.com.*

HELP YOUR FRIENDS SURVIVE!

Order extra copies of *You Can Keep the Damn China!*, or one of our other books.

Please send me:

_____ copies of *"You Can Keep the Damn China!"* (@$13.95)

_____ copies of *How to Lose 9,000 Lbs. (or Less)* (@$13.95)

_____ copies of *How to Survive Your Teenager* (@$13.95)

_____ copies of *How to Survive a Move* (@$13.95)

_____ copies of *How to Survive Your Marriage* (@$13.95)

_____ copies of *How to Survive Your Baby's First Year* (@$12.95)

_____ copies of *How to Survive Dating* (@$12.95)

_____ copies of *How to Survive Your Freshman Year* (@$12.95)

Please add $3.00 for shipping and handling for one book, and $1.00 for each additional book. Georgia residents add 4% sales tax. Kansas residents add 5.3% sales tax. Payment must accompany orders. Please allow three weeks for delivery.

My check for $_____ is enclosed.

Please charge my __ Visa __ MasterCard __ American Express

Name _____

Organization _____

Address _____

City/State/Zip _____

Phone _____E-mail _____

Credit card # _____

Exp. Date _____Signature _____

Please make checks payable to HUNDREDS OF HEADS BOOKS, LLC

HELP WRITE THE NEXT Hundreds of Heads® SURVIVAL GUIDE!

Tell us your story about a life experience, and what lesson you learned from it. If we use your story in one of our books, we'll send you a free copy. Use this card or visit **www.hundredsofheads.com**.

Here's my story/advice on surviving

❏ **A NEW JOB** (years working:_____ profession/job:_____)

❏ **A MOVE** (# of times you've moved:____) ❏ **A DIET** (# of lbs. lost in best diet: ____)

❏ **A TEENAGER** (ages/sexes of your children: _____)

❏ **DIVORCE** (# of times married: _____ # of times divorced:_____)

❏ _____ **OTHER TOPIC** (you pick)

Name: _____City/State: _____

❏ Use my name ❏ Use my initials only ❏ Anonymous

(Note: Your entry in the book may also include city/state and the descriptive information above.)

_____
Signature

How should we contact you *(this will not be published or shared)*:

e-mail: _____ other: _____

Please fax to 212-937-2220 or mail to:

HUNDREDS OF HEADS BOOKS, LLC
#230
2221 Peachtree Road, Suite D
Atlanta, Georgia 30309

Your story/advice:

VISIT WWW.HUNDREDSOFHEADS.COM

Do you have something interesting to say about marriage, your in-laws, dieting, holding a job, or one of life's other challenges?

Help humanity—share your story!

 Get published in our next book!

 Find out about the upcoming titles in the HUNDREDS OF HEADS™ survival guide series!

 Read up-to-the-minute advice on many of life's challenges!

 Sign up to become an interviewer for one of the next HUNDREDS OF HEADS® survival guides!

Visit www.hundredsofheads.com today!

Other Books from HUNDREDS OF HEADS™ BOOKS

HOW TO SURVIVE YOUR FRESHMAN YEAR . . . by Hundreds of Sophomores, Juniors, and Seniors Who Did (and some things to avoid, from a few dropouts who didn't)™
(April 2004; ISBN 0-9746292-0-0)

HOW TO SURVIVE DATING . . . by Hundreds of Happy Singles Who Did (and some things to avoid, from a few broken hearts who didn't)™
(October 2004; ISBN 0-9746292-1-9)

HOW TO SURVIVE YOUR BABY'S FIRST YEAR . . . by Hundreds of Happy Parents Who Did (and some things to avoid, from a few who barely made it)™
(January 2005; ISBN 0-9746292-2-7)

HOW TO SURVIVE YOUR MARRIAGE . . . by Hundreds of Happy Couples Who Did (and some things to avoid, from a few ex-spouses who didn't)™
(February 2005; 0-9746292-4-3)

HOW TO SURVIVE A MOVE . . . by Hundreds of Happy Dwellers Who Did (and some things to avoid, from a few who haven't unpacked yet)™
(April 2005; 0-9746292-5-1)

HOW TO SURVIVE YOUR TEENAGER . . . by Hundreds of Still-Sane Parents Who Did (and some things to avoid, from a few whose kids drove them nuts)™
(May 2005; ISBN 0-9746292-3-5)

HOW TO LOSE 9,000 LBS. (OR LESS): Advice from 516 Dieters Who Did
(January 2006; ISBN 0-9746292-8-6)

About the Editors

ROBERT J. NACHSHIN, a certi-
fied family law specialist,
represents celebrities in music,
film, television, and sports as
well as high-net-worth individuals. Based in West Los Angeles,
CA, Nachshin is co-author of *I
Do, You Do . . . But Just Sign
Here: A Quick and Easy Guide
to Cohabitation, Prenuptial and
Postnuptial Agreements.* He is
best known for his precedent-
setting win in the Barry Bonds
prenuptial case, in which
Nachshin and his partner, Scott
Weston, after a 10-year battle,
prevailed at the California
Supreme Court level. To read
more about Robert J. Nachshin,
visit www.nwdivorce.com.

JENNIFER BRIGHT REICH is a
special editor and headhunter
for the Hundreds of Heads
Survival Guide series. With more
than 10 years of book-publishing
experience, she has contributed
to more than 70 books. She lives
in Hellertown, Pennsylvania,
with her second husband and
new baby.